*Maximum Security Ward
and Other Poems*

Persea Lamplighter Titles
Essential Texts in Poetry and Poetics

M.L. Rosenthal, General Editor

Ramon Guthrie

Maximum
Security Ward

and Other Poems

edited, with an introduction, by
Sally M. Gall

Persea Books
New York

Text and introduction copyright © 1984 by Sally M. Gall.
Foreword copyright © 1984 by M. L. Rosenthal.
Materials included in this volume first appeared in book form in *Graffiti,* ©
1957, 1958, 1959 by Ramon Guthrie; in *Asbestos Phoenix,* © 1968 by Ramon
Guthrie; and in *Maximum Security Ward 1964-1970,* © 1968, 1969, 1970 by
Ramon Guthrie.

The editor gratefully acknowledges the help of Dartmouth College, Hanover,
New Hampshire; of Mr. Kenneth C. Cramer, Archivist, Dartmouth College
Library; and of Professor Stephen G. Nichols, Jr., in making this edition possible.

Library of Congress Cataloging in Publication Data

Guthrie, Ramon, 1896-
    Maximum security ward and other poems.

    (Lamplighter titles)
    Includes bibliographical references and index.
    1. Gall, Sally M.   II. Title.   III. Series.
PS3513.U875A6   1984   811'.52   83-22067
ISBN 0-89255-079-1
ISBN 0-89255-080-5 (pbk.)

Manufactured in the United States of America.
First Printing.

for
Sally Hughes-Schrader
and
in memory of
Alexander Laing

Foreword

It is pure joy to be able to launch the new Lamplighter series with a selection of Ramon Guthrie's verse, including the whole of his masterpiece: *Maximum Security Ward*. To make Guthrie available to all readers once more, in this carefully and lovingly edited volume, would alone justify the series as an undertaking to provide indispensable books of poetry and poetic criticism at a time of absurd confusion in the poetic "scene."

Ramon Guthrie (1896-1973) was a splendid star in our poetic skies, but criticism fixed its whimsical telescope on him hardly at all. One recalls with enduring amazement the difficulties this endlessly engaging poet, so humorous and painfully alive and truly accomplished, met in publishing his work. *Graffiti*, the rigorously winnowed collection of the work of years, did not appear until he was sixty-three. *Asbestos Phoenix* appeared nine years later, and *Maximum Security Ward* two years further on. Each volume had to find a new publisher, flashed briefly into view, received high praise here and there, and soon dropped out of print. Why? For no good reason, really—only the familiar general indifference to the real thing and identification of publicity with reputation.

Self-publicizing was emphatically not Guthrie's forte. He belonged to no elite group on the make but led an isolated life as a Dartmouth professor, taking holidays when he could in his beloved Paris. Witty and daring as he shows himself in his poems, he was shy and diffident in his relations with the "larger" literary world. Ideally this should not have mattered. What counts in the republic of letters—ideally—is one thing only: the quality of what you write. Essentially, Guthrie lived by this principle, the basic driving principle of art; and in *Maximum Security Ward* he acts it out literally and symbolically. For one thing, he makes a vital poetry out of his own mortal illness and agonies. For another, he dreams himself into the state of a great primitive cave-painter who, unsupported by companions and laboring without recognition, creates a mystically realistic work that transcends his own time and condition. A gifted painter himself, and an admirer of painters like Cranach and Delvaux who fuse power with fanciful imagination, Guthrie created a body of poems sharing these artists' audaciously earthy and psychologically penetrating vision.

Perhaps—it just may be—that ugly factor, politics, prevented Guthrie's full recognition. He is richly and responsibly of the humanistic Left, as much so as Pound and Eliot and Yeats were of the Right, and yet not at all of the dogmatically tendentious world of the most popular poetic ideologues of our time from Ginsberg to Rich and Baraka. One glance at a poem like "Polar Bear" or "Homage to Paul Delvaux" would dissipate any easy preconception about the work of this leftist, illusionless veteran of the two great wars. He was not of any poetic-political "camp"; he was simply a finely responsive poet who, like the later William Carlos Williams and the almost forgotten Kenneth Fearing, reveals—in Keats's word—the penetralia of a lifetime of American experience.

With scrupulous scholarship and an intimate knowledge of Guthrie's *oeuvre*, Dr. Sally M. Gall has selected his best work for inclusion in this edition. Her special sense of his aura began in conversations during his last years—conversations that reverberate in her finely indicative introduction to his art and poetic development. She brings to bear as well the results of her deep studies of modern poetic sequences, to which she has occasion to refer in the course of her introduction. *Maximum Security Ward* is clearly an important exemplar of this crucial modern genre.

Move over, Lowell, Plath, Berryman, Olson, etc! An older confrere and even truer child of Walt now marches along with you *visibly*, shedding his natural glow of wry irony and quiet heroism over that famous open road, which still lies before us and still invites ever further exploration.

M.L.R.

Contents

from *Asbestos Phoenix* (1968)

Maximum Security Ward (1970)

Part One

Introduction

   Lovers of language who are newcomers to Ramon Guthrie's poetry are in for those small shocks of happy surprise that make for poetry at its most energetic and enjoyable. They may chance upon our modern troubadour's bravura curse on every future lover of his "cool and agile" mistress:

> through unabridged eternity may he
> grub fallow memory fruitless to conjure up
> this smooth knoll of your shoulder,
> this cwm of flank, this moss-delineated quite
> un-Platonic cave.
>
> (p. 40)

Or upon the delighted vignette of a sleeping eight-year-old:

> Eyelashes against contour of a
> cheek and nose tip
>   coiled limber spine
> sprawled disrupted skein of
>   elbows   knees   shins
>   sneakered feet
> mane whose pendant weight would be
>   wasted on a pillow
>
> (p. 63)

Or upon the hilarious, pedantic idiocy of "The Neutrino and Mr. Brinsley":

> Take the neutrino—of which we know the less
> the more we know about it. Nevertheless
> the neutrino, in a manner of speaking, *is*—

though its manner of speaking is definitely not
that of Palgrave's *Golden Treasury*.

> You may
> expound cosmology to a flower in a crannied wall,
> try to convince a lark that it never was a bird. . . .

(p. 67)

And upon a great many more moments that sparkle with wit even
when the perception is essentially tragic, as in this wry reminiscence
of youth's belief in its own invulnerability:

> . . . death no more
> real for me than for the fool squirrel
> racing to throw a body block
> on an oncoming truck.

(p. 100)

Guthrie's poetry is deeply—movingly—funny, tragic, sar-
donic, sweet-spirited, and brave in a way that makes one rejoice in
being human and in being privileged to share his poetic universe.
That exuberant cosmos is peopled with mermaids, satyrs, clowns,
and polar bears; with an asbestos phoenix, a stalled meteor, and a
very Guthrian trio of Magi ("Are there in these place one inn?");
with archangels and troubadours; with members of the *Résistance*
and Paleolithic cave painters—indeed, with heroes and artists of all
sorts and conditions; and with "ordinary" people humbly and lovingly
seen as quite extraordinary:

> What did he mean (this insurance executive) by
> "The common man is the common hero?"

(p. 133)

So even an insurance executive (in this instance, to be sure, none
other than Wallace Stevens) finds a place in Guthrie's universe,
along with such denizens of the *Golden Treasury* as Tennyson and

Shelley. Guthrie was a very contemporary American poet; neverthe-
less, he read deeply and well within the English and American
tradition, and his outstanding handling of sound textures, especially
in his remarkably fluent and flexible free verse, reflects this immer-
sion.

Further, Guthrie had an expert's knowledge of the French
poetic tradition. He was a professor of French at Dartmouth, a
compiler of standard French anthologies, a translator, and a Fran-
cophile who lived in France for much of the 1920s, maintained
close ties with the artistic community there all his life, and married
a Frenchwoman. In his own poetry French is resorted to tactfully,
only when his sense of the exact word allows no other course. His
jeu d'esprit "Gemini" ponders this kind of decision with light-hearted
exasperation, citing such crucial pairings as "woman" and "femme,"
"homme" and "man," and "amour" and "love":

> One of them is much more
> something or other than the other:
> They are as different as
> to die and mourir
> Though how to define
> their differences either only
> Dieu knows or God sait.
>
> (p. 10)

Appearances to the contrary, it is unlikely that "God" and
"Dieu" slipped into this poem as incidental embellishments. An
intense concern with what constitutes true divinity in thoroughly
human terms shapes some of Guthrie's most powerful poetry. Born
before the turn of the century—in January 1896—and raised by a
"truly pious" mother, whatever inclinations he might have had to-
wards an easy, unquestioning belief seem to have been thoroughly
shattered by the moral and psychological pressures of our modern
war age. He served in two world wars and coped as best he could
with the eras of Korea and Vietnam, protesting this last with particu-
lar vehemence. When he died in November 1973, at the age of

seventy-seven, the cease-fire agreement had been in effect for less than a year. His grief and horror at American involvement in Vietnam are abundantly clear in the last two selections from *Asbestos Phoenix* and in such momentarily disillusioned passages in *Maximum Security Ward* as this acidly contemptuous dismissal of the merits of being human:

> No, not even for the laughs. The race of
> napalm Santa Clauses!
> Sheep herded by glib lies that greed concocts,
> he-harpies safely out of sight and sound
> cheerily showering some thousand tons of bombs
> on the innocent helpless to strike back,
> pointless despoilers and defilers of what
> might elsewise be a fairly pleasant world.
>
> (p. 123)

It is precisely this kind of savage misbehavior that raises the question in "Fiercer Than Evening Wolves..." of whether there might be "relief in having a God to hate." But in Guthrie's moral universe guilt rests squarely on human shoulders. Any balancing of evil by good must come, too, from the same sources: from all those who "bear witness . . . to human dignity." From one perspective the forty-nine-poem *Maximum Security Ward*, Guthrie's most important work and a major contribution to the genre of the modern poetic sequence,* both explores and "bears witness" to the nature of this "human dignity." It is a celebration of those who, in their varied and sometimes surprising fashions, have brought back "secrets for changing life." Frequently these are artists—painters, sculptors, writers, musicians—but they may be scientists, revolutionaries, or any free spirits who have refused to submit to the tyranny of received ideas, or of political power, or indeed of any human limitation—including the indignities imposed by one's aging, all-too-mortal flesh.

---

*For a full discussion of this modern form of the long poem, see M. L. Rosenthal and Sally M. Gall, *The Modern Poetic Sequence: The Genius of Modern Poetry* (New York: Oxford University Press, 1983).

The dramatic situation of *Maximum Security Ward*—an old and physically helpless patient in an intensive care unit—gives rise to plenty of indignities. Nevertheless, our poet wields a barbed pen, and his sequence should be required reading for every medical student and hospital staff member. The satirical "Red-Headed Intern, Taking Notes," for example, projects the utter exasperation an entering patient—who may be in pain, or frightened, or both—feels at being asked inane questions by a cheerily unconcerned youngster: "No history of zombi-ism in the immediate family? . . . No recent intercourse with a rabbit?" The atmosphere of prison *cum* insane asylum is exuberantly compounded by the nonsensical jargon Guthrie coins in "Scene: A Bedside in the Witches' Kitchen" for the activities of more senior staff:

> DOCTOR *to his retinue of interns and residents*:
> Obvious ptoritus of the drabia.
> Although the prizzle presents no sign of rabies,
> note this pang in the upper diaphrosis.
> When kicked there hard enough, the patient utters,
> "Yoof!" and curls up like a cutworm.
> I prescribe bedcheck every hour on the hour
> with intensive catalepsis. (*Exeunt.*)
>
> (p. 94)

Like Yeats, Guthrie did not take kindly to growing old. However, his more humane and essentially more humble vision embraces the ludicrous aspects of the aging process and yields comedy of a high order, making believable the triumph in *Maximum Security Ward* of the human spirit over bodily pain and humiliation. Guthrie belongs to that tragically small company of poets who have done superb work in their seventies or beyond—poets with the power, and courage, to distill in their art their intimate experience of the trials and glories of old age.

It is even more unusual, however, for a poet to do by far his best work so late in life. Guthrie's early publications were sensitive to modernist currents but not really of international caliber: *Trobar*

Clus (S4N Society, 1923), *A World Too Old* (Doran, 1927), and a little chapbook, *Scherzo from a Poem To Be Entitled The Proud City* (The Arts Press, 1933). More interesting, actually, are his two novels from the same period: *Marcabrun* (Doran, 1926), based on the life of the troubadour, and *Parachute* (Harcourt, 1928), one of the first aviation novels. Still, there is no doubt that Guthrie from the beginning had all the instincts of a poet—some of his translations from the Provençal are quite fine—but he found very little salvageable in its original form. Two self-derisive lines from *Scherzo*, however, are repeated in *Graffiti*: "The voice of the Lord spoke out of a whirlwind. / I answered Him out of a cyclone cellar" (p. 25). An unpublished long poem from 1938, "Instead of Abel"*—written in response to the Spanish Civil War and unremittingly political in its thrust—fared slightly better. Guthrie chose three of its sections for *Graffiti*; the best one, "Postlude: For Goya," is included here (p. 16). In general, "Instead of Abel" and *Scherzo* are of interest mainly as exercises in longer poetic structures that found their culmination in *Maximum Security Ward*.

During the 1930s and 1940s Guthrie painted, taught Proust—he has admitted that once he had read Proust he gave up all thought of being a novelist—and kept very quiet about his poetry. Then, in the 1950s, periodicals gave space to his evocative clown dancing in the clearing by night (p. 4), his mermaids cavorting in Maine (p. 13), his provocative giraffes (p. 25), his modern Europa (p. 26), and other fantastic creatures. And at the end of the decade *Graffiti* (Macmillan, 1959)—his first full-sized collection since 1927—appeared, its highly imaginative poems spinning bumptiously on an axis provided by the motif of the poet as tragicomic clown.

After his retirement from full-time teaching in 1963—the occasion of a festschrift† that includes poems, essays, reminiscences, and illustrations by friends at home and abroad—he chose to devote

---

*"Instead of Abel" is among the Guthrie papers in the Archives of the Dartmouth College Library.

†*Ramon Guthrie Kaleidoscope* (Stinehour Press, 1963). Among some thirty-five items are contributions by Dilys and Alexander Laing, Tristan Tzara, Malcolm Cowley, M. L. Rosenthal, Norman Fitts, George Seldes, Alexander Calder, Stephen Nichols, and Laurette Véza.

more and more time to poetry, despite acute bouts of illness—"Then this last time, so close they thought it best / to take the copyright in my wife's name" (p. 99). The reference is apparently to *Asbestos Phoenix* (Funk & Wagnalls, 1968), a versatile collection with such beautifully crafted poems as "Brittle as Threads of Glass" (p. 39), "L'Enfance de la Sirène" (p. 53), and "Homage to Paul Delvaux" (p. 55). Of particular interest also are Guthrie's deft handling of the comic in such poems as "Dialogue with the Sphinx" (p. 72) and "The Magi" (p. 75), his remarkable fusion of the personal and mythic in "Pattern for a Brocade Shroud" (p. 42), his increasing concern with the United States' Asian entanglements ("Some of Us Must Remember"—p. 80—and "Scherzo for a Dirge"—p. 82) and the "Marsyas in the Intensive Care Ward" section, comprising four poems that would find their proper place in *Maximum Security Ward* (Farrar, Straus & Giroux, 1970).

Alexander Laing, a Dartmouth colleague, fellow poet, and dear friend whose generous assistance Guthrie acknowledged in the dedications or notes to all his late books, recorded something of the effort that went into the completion of *Maximum Security Ward*, which appeared when Guthrie was seventy-four. The portrait he draws* is of a desperately ill human being struggling—whatever the cost—to fulfill a contract he has made with himself. "Be ashamed to die," Horace Mann said more than a hundred years ago, "until you have won some victory for humanity." *Maximum Security Ward* is such a victory, not least because it celebrates private victories: the work performed because, to be fully human, one must do it—whether or not it will ever be acknowledged. Thus Guthrie gives us the lusty and superb twelfth-century troubadour Arnaut Daniel, doubting for the moment that his art and name will endure:

Aï! given a few springs more and even the spawn
of my own loins won't ever have heard my name.
Their mammies will have told them,

---

*"Pain, Memory and Glory: The Poetry of Ramon Guthrie" (*Carleton Miscellany*, Summer 1970).

"Your pappy was a travelin' man," or
"You are the offspring of a foreign dignitary
who, hearing of my beauty, sent his emissaries . . ."

(p. 168)

And he summons up a prehistoric cave painter who, in "The Making of the Bear," battles to complete a work that may never be seen:

> but in winding scapes of underground
> where no sun's light has ever shone,
> finger may touch the lash
> of open eye unseen.
>
>   There
> in that total lack of light
> is where my bear is.
> No one will ever see him
> but he still
> is there.

(p. 195)

But the poet's supreme creation is Marsyas-Guthrie, the exultant/despairing, pugnacious/gentle, scathing/compassionate, vaunting/humble protagonist of *Maximum Security Ward*, who at last relinquishes his life-long quarrel with violent, errant gods and manages a very human victory:

> My name is Marsyas. I played a flute.
> Forget that silly challenge. I played it best alone,
> sitting on a rock or sprawled on banks of wolf's-foot,
> checkerberries.
> A chipmunk now and then would sit up and listen . . .

(p. 189)

This solitary flautist becomes the wondering man who, in the closing poem of *Maximum Security Ward*, catches so accurately the creative spirit at its most intense—capable of evoking, whatever our frailties and failings, a veritable "Dawn beyond all limit of horizon."

Truly this poet could meet death without shame.

Suffern, New York   *Sally M. Gall*
August 1983

Maximum Security Ward and Other Poems

from
Graffiti

(1959)

Rance nuit de la peau quand sur moi vous passiez,
Ne sachant pas, ingrat! que c'était tout mon sacre,
Ce fard noyé dans l'eau perfide des glaciers.

Mallarmé: *Le Pitre châtié*

Recipe and Introduction

You take a friendly vampire going about its slant-eyed
business. You take a busy banshee yowling loud and clear.
You take a plump tarantula no doubt and a can tied
to a gray ape's tail. You take a girl like Lilith
in a blanket by a campfire (can she
stop her prowling in her shroud and snitching beer?)
You take a blizzard's trail severed but still twitching.
You make a cairn upon a barren hill and stake
a sign nearby (the letter killeth)
Saying *KEEP OUT* to catch some beastie's eye
and start it itching to creep *in*. And there
you have a recipe for brewing—
not trouble, no, but something close akin.
You take a doorknob dug among the rubble
of an ancient Kymric village: turn it and walk in.

The Clown: He Dances
in the Clearing by Night

He took his wig off, with his sleeve
wiped painted snigger from his face
and did a dance you'd not believe . . .
with easy-jointed limpid pace
wove through such figures as the eye
could scarcely follow, whistling slow
a tune of scant variety
like whispers on a piccolo.

The Tyger in his forest stared,
chin sunk upon his powered paws
while pirouette and caper dared
the awesome sinews of the Laws
his stripèd humors improvise—
Immutabilities laid down
by conclaves of eternities—
revoked an instant by the Clown.

He danced the twittering of quails
and dolphins' pleasure in the sea
and planets screaming on their rails
of finely drawn infinity.
Then naked, having cast aside
motley of Time and Space and Number,
he glided silent through the wide
vistas of the Tyger's slumber.

The Ruts

"Ornières"
Rimbaud

Were the ruts already there
before the chariots passed
driven by teamsters with their denim legs
showing beneath their togas?

There were plump
pipe-clayed stallions with yellow
red and blue
pompons braided in their manes
and fringed pillions on their rumps
gilded wooden Tritons blowing horns
and for the children
cornucopias spilling hard
bright sugar candies
and for the grown-ups
pink and white mermaids
their breasts spouting real wine.

On one float Moses
stood in effigy with his brazen serpent
on another Peter with his crowing cock
and Balaam and his neighbor's ox and the
calliope
mooming like Gabriel's trumpet and
Michael slaying a steam-snorting dragon
and a woolly tiger whose eyes flashed on and off
and an even woollier lamb
that tinkled hurdy-gurdy pastorals
when grave clowns with shepherds' crooks
and gabled caps churned its tail.

When the parade had passed

and the last heavy wain
had lurched beneath the crest
all that remained under the scudding clouds
was this track
gouged across an upland heath
the water stagnant in the ruts
glinting red in the sunset
a curlew's whimper

     silence.

It was then that the three Norns
each tall as birch-tops
ribs like coopers' hoops
and rawhide bellies tipped
with scant boar-bristle tufts
stood for a moment their mumbling gums
sucking incantations from the wind.

  Toward nightfall the stragglers came
haggard
one by one
scanning the earth's edge
sniffing the uneasy wind. Some few perhaps
succumbed and lapped the water in the ruts.
Then one lifted his voice
Thalassa Thalassa
No sea in sound or sight
they knew the whiff of it
they had been sea-bred men.

Dead, How to Become It

> The Reverend James Guthrie was executed in 1661 and
> his head affixed over Edinburgh's Nether Bow Port. His
> cousin William wrote a number of edifying tracts.

1

William said (or so the legend goes)
to James: "*You* will die a proud death
with a rope about your neck and folk
looking up at you—while I
shall die whining upon a little straw."
    And it happened as he said, for James at least:
of William's death there is no record.
A man dies as he dies. Only the saint
chooses his death as he has chosen life,
is master of his coming and his going.

2

I shall hear singing and shall not make out the tune,
I shall remember the fisher girl
on the quai at Volo and not recall
the pride of her neck
nor her brown feet set
on the ancient coping stones
stained with the sepia squirts of octopi.

    I shall follow in a dream of empty eye
the eagle wheeling below the domed
summit in the Cévennes where
long before Caesar and Vercingetorix
a stone-age temple stood,
three slabs of wind-gouged stone,
but I shall have forgotten the meaning of pride.

3

There are those to whom

death is the snapping of a violin string
strained to too shrill an ecstasy.
Then there are also
young men's deaths
like a puppy's lunge parting a frayed leash.

There are those who die
on a steep rocky path, proud in their defeat,
spending their last strength to drag themselves
to the last bend but one
before the horizon,
knowing that there is no horizon.

(I think of the maquisards of the Vercors,
girls and boys going into battle
with clubs and scythes against
tanks and paratroopers: their last message,
"Adieu. Nous mourons en Français.
Vous êtes des salauds." And the planes
that could have saved them
sitting idle on landing-mats,
grounded by old men's unwieldy deliberations,
an hour's flight away.)

4

Beside these there are those whose death
is the muted continuity
of a querulous dream.

To lull the whimper of my absence
I shall tell myself bedtime stories,
sing myself lullabies:

"Hush, you died at Teruel.
Hush, you lie by the Ebro.
Sleep, you fell clicking an empty pistol

at the gliders in the Vercors
or blasted by the close-range volley
that drilled your blood
into the prison wall of Mont-Valérien.
    As you name each place,
forget that you were never there
(not at the time, at least)
forget that you died of a useless
ingrown impatience and an equally
fruitless
accumulation of monotony."

Gemini

Twins in French are jumeaux
Jument put into English is a mare
To drink is boire
but they are not the same.
They may *mean* the same:
that is as close as they can ever get:
always one is cooler, sharper,
grosser, downier, more immediate
or less substantial than the other.

There is woman and there is femme
and *they* are not the same
even when you apply
both words to the same person—

though, all in all, un homme
is not too unlike a man (functionally, at least)
And there is amour and love
What either of them is I cannot say
except that they are not
identical
One of them is much more
something or other than the other:
They are as different as
to die and mourir
Though how to define
their differences either only
Dieu knows or God sait.

The Clown: Hurrah for the Petrified Forest

So jammervoll klagt kein Wild.
Wagner

Centaurs and satyrs are gone. To that
I am quite reconciled. They were no kith
or kin of mine anyway. But what of those other
fantastic creatures who, like to me as brothers,
free-swimming, once roamed the earth?
What of them?
                    Oh, the beautiful desert!
Not a thing grows here! Not a fig! Not a thistle.
Not an expository blade of grass,
not a dove, not a serpent.
How perfectly like one's worst imaginings. What an ideal

setting and habitat for one's bleakest dreads.
Just look: my eyes are pockets of alkali,
my limbs are chunks of petrified wood. Visitors
are requested not to deface them.

I am one of the natural curiosities of the place:
on clear days at sixty paces
you can hear the fibres of me scream.

On a Bare Mountain in the Cévennes

Here it is far too high for cock-
crow to rise or any light
from valley hamlet to be seen.

Only the cool or warm of rock
under scant scurf sets season right.
Such clouds as skim above are lean

with eerie vigil, scavengers
of close-gleaned ether. Eagle and hawk
wheel far below this barren crest.

Black leopards, Lucifer's avengers,
here pad in pairs, scorn stealth to stalk
Chronos' daughters. Here come to rest

the leaden seraphs of despair

which *chose* their fall—where not the blast
of Gabriel's trumpet singing doom

could wake a shudder in the air.
Here might a man's bones find at last
in fierce serenity their tomb,

his blood libation to the Light
above remorse or joy or grief
or pity, silence be his shroud

outside of time, by wordless rite
redeemed of yearning or relief

—save that Lucifer is proud.

Mousikè

> "By *poetry I mean . . . that intercommunication between
> the inner being of things and the inner being of the
> human Self which is a kind of divination . . . another
> name for what Plato called* mousikè."
>   Jacques Maritain

That which deciphers yet unwritten runes
as surely as an iron filing homes to its
place in the pattern of a magnetic field

obedient to a symmetry that *is* not till it finds it

That which impudently cuts itself a peplum
out of night and wears it in the market place at noon
where it sets up as an interpreter
   without a common language

That which overhears the hummingbird's waspish reply
to the humble solicitations of the daisy

That which trues the pitch of the trumpet vine

That which re-fights the battle of Jericho and the stones
go scrambling back into their places and
to Joshua's unalloyed annoyance
start sprouting silver turrets

That which destroys bridges in order to be
on both sides of the river at once
and builds bridges as it goes
by destroying them

Is its own indivisible incongruity
reflected but not caught   on any page.

Mermaids in Maine

That spring's neap   tide brought
a phenomenal catch
of mermaids. They were so cheap

that you could buy a batch
almost for the asking—
big, small, middling, all   with neat white basking
midriffs. Some folks bought
them to fry in butter   and some to utter rude
noises at them and see them flutter.
Some liked them stewed   and some to keep
in gilded cages   and hear them cheep
and try to guess their ages.

There *were* hitches   so to say: tourists
would not believe that they existed;
calling them "sirens" troubled purists;
scales obviated any need for breeches,
but parish ladies in dismay rose
and insisted   on boleros.

Most of them could be taught to talk a bit,
say, "Pretty please"   or "Pretty Poll"
or a few swearwords in Portuguese.
Others would only chirp or squawk a bit,
and some were dumb.   Slaughtered, flayed
and stuffed, they made
an attractive and unusual doll.

One crude codger, lobsterman of Bar,
for sheer libido   went as far
as having one tattooed (a lustrous creature
musky golden as a daylily)
with questionable, if not exactly lewd,
mottoes like "Oh, you kiddo!"
Of evenings he played   lotto or checkers with her
yet never quite could teach her
not to slither   scalily
off his lap,   so he attests.

Caught young and fed on pap   and spayed,
their otherwise buddingly   little chests
stayed flat as a boy's   so that for a season
Miss Meeker's Antiquity Shop displayed
them with propriety and success
as pets or toys
till suddenly   and for no known reason
the catch fell off.   In a week or less
it came to a stop,   since when,
except as now and then   you'll find one drowned
in a mackerel seine   or lobster pot
in the cool of the moon, there is almost not
a mermaid found   on the coast of Maine.

The Clown: A Natural History

Meeting a chattering
chipmunk I took flight.

Fleeing the chipmunk
well into the night
I scuffled on a cobra.

Scattering leaves he whipped
into a stalk of menace.

Fleeing the cobra's hiss I tripped
into a stony pit.

A lion let forth a startled roar
and spit.

Fleeing the lion then as
I had fled before
from other things
I ran until I sank
exhausted, fell asleep
beside an ant hill
hidden in the rank
deep
grass where I am lying still—
stricken past mattering
by a million venomed stings.

Postlude: For Goya

(1938)

A bloody day subsided: the volcano's lips
cool to slag, its glow a tracery
faint against the sky. (Oh, there is still
a sky.) How different this calm from peace.
We are too shattered now to count our losses.
What is there left but loss? Who still can hope
that because we fought, others will fight,
because we were broken that earth still holds
some traces of a destiny?

We are alone tonight, each of us alone,
before and after a storm, breathing in a lull,
caught in a bight of ashy slackness.
A broad lightning painted on the sky shows livid
two skinned bulls, motionless, backed off
from goring one another. We crouch
behind a knoll of pumice and the dry clouds lie
so near above us we could reach a hand
almost to touch them. There is dust in our mouths.
Beads of useless power
exude like gum from the earth and sounds
are sucked from our lips by silence. At our feet
the bones of a buzzard lie beside
the shadowy fox's bones that stalked it.
You stare at a dry hollow and your lips
peel back from your teeth
and your shoulders mean laughter
remembering it lately was a brook.
(We must not shrink to gauge our madness,
the heat-sprung brain and fingers brittle as
scorched ivory, eyes with certain visions
baked into them.) This is not an end,
only an interlude: after a while
we will creep forth and search among the crevices
for seeds and cover them with dust
and try for tears to quicken them.
Remember only this is not an end.
We cannot win—though we perhaps have won
if we can only believe
that this is not the end.

The Clown's Report on Satyrs

On the hoof or dead, a satyr weighs
about the single same. They mingle
with goddesses and singe themselves in flame
that they ignite with steady gaze
while they recite the name of One
who in the olden days
slept on Naxos' shingle,
and they are golden ruddy in the sun
and hold themselves aloof.
A satyr on the hoof is fleet.
Slaughtered, their dark red meat is strong.

All the King's Horses

1

After the decline of the Visigothic Empire
the world relaxed into a state of intermittent chaos:
flowers replaced blood sacrifice on altars,
solecisms cropped up in epitaphs and established values
fell into disrepute. Into the breach
stepped the Satrap of Ampersand, he who had dealt
so firmly with the revolt of the palace dustmen.
He levied heavy taxes on indigence and illiteracy
and drew up intricate forms on which returns
must be filed (though pending the invention of movable type,
they could not yet be printed). He took

credit where credit was due and erected
a number of obelisks commemorating himself
as the saviour of Christian Civilization.

2

With the failure of the treaty of Bithynia to guarantee
longevity, the Varangian Guard issued an ultimatum
demanding the *jus primae noctis* for sextons.
Yorick could have come out of retirement and handled the
                                        situation
but Yorick was not only, as he himself attested,
senile but long since dead. Nevertheless a coalition
of dedicated oligarchs acting in his name
took over the power and did the best they could.
They banned mead and artificial insemination
if and when it should occur and decreed
menhirs and triumphal arches to themselves for saving
the universe for posterity and incidentally preserving
the integrity of Christian civilization.

3

After the Great Fall when, in view of the conceded inability
of the military to cope with the disaster,
a patient concourse of thinkers and craftsmen at length
not only did put Humpty Dumpty together again
but re-established the Peace of Eden, the world
began to drift into an era of complacency—
lovers lay night long in gardens, travelers
went freely where they would; Swede and Bantu,
Tuareg and Gael met together as brothers;
thinkers spoke their thoughts honestly without fear—
till up there sprang a Movement of Integral Regeneration
under the energetic leadership of such heroes as
the Reverend Chasuble, General Warhead, and young Mr. Pluto-
        flap.
They smithered both Humpty and his wall to irretrievable bits,

turned gardens into launching pads and—WHAM—
    BRO-ther! Did that ever wrap it up
      for christyumcilivizashum!

"And They Said, Go to, Let Us Build Us a City . . ."

Genesis 11:4

Here I will plant my stakes to build a city—
this is the very site I have always been looking for—
to be an Ecbatana, Samarkand or Avalon.
The principal café with broad terrasse
under catalpas will stand here, and down cobbled
side-street under sotto-portici
will be the little bistrot with a bosomy patronne
behind the counter and marble-topped tables that a man
can draw doodles on. Yonder beyond that crest
will be the park with ibises and lilypads
and bullfrogs—somehow we're going to have to get a river:
perhaps for the time being a second-hand one would do—
and a rocky place for onagers to gallop,
rock python bask and jerboas skit about.
We might as well have also a few white camels
with red tassels on their halters and a refrigerated pool
for polar bears.

           The nearest airfield will be
at Karachi or Keflavik, the nearest autoroute
in Joplin, Missouri, and the nearest night-club

in Frederikshaab. The only motor vehicle
will be in the museum along with a chastity-belt,
a neon sign and other by-then-forgotten
instruments of vexation.

                      The town will have
one plumber (named Chris, I think) who will always come
when he says he will and invariably find that there is nothing
needed but a new washer—which he happens to have in his
    pocket.
There will be sacred groves and gods galore
from Priapus and Kali to the Black Virgin of Le Puy
and the same officiants for all of them.
There will be cucking-stools for diplomats
and prompt euthanasia for those who have attained
the grade of elder statesman.

     Eventually, of course,
     there will be need
     of grapes and hops and grass
     and soil of sorts to grow them in:
     not even lichen
     finds nurture on this flinty tor:
     as of now, its only attributes
     are remoteness and solitude—
     which building here a city might dispel.

Footsteps in the Stairway

If I am to read the thousand pages of
    this monstrous tome
whose cover, straining all night long,
    I only now have opened,
I must do it quickly: it is nearly dawn.
A first sparrow cheeps in the gutter of the mansard
    outside my window:
the filament of the single light-bulb
    hung from the ceiling
cools to a dull red loop. The characters
in a vaguely Gothic font and in a tongue
    I do not recognize
scramble like frantic ants back to their places.

Without my having even heard a creak
    in the stairway,
the landlady is knocking sharply at my door.
Gaunt as a larch, her parchment belly taut
between the flanges of her pelvis,
she stands on the landing, so tall
    the lintel hides her face.
Behind her, naked as herself, her three
roly-poly daughters with chapped red knees
    and ankles
simper and hitch their hips,
    eyes modestly downcast.

The eviction notice is engraved on vellum
and bears the signature and seals
of three Lords Chancellor
    dead long before I was born.

Steps are mounting the stairway:

as if they did not know as well as I,
simultaneously the three daughters turn and lean
far over the bannister to peer.
Tattooed on pudgy bottoms are their names:
Clotho   Lachesis   Atropos

       I stride to close the cover of the book:
       a breeze has done it for me.

For the first time I notice that a tocsin
that has been tolling all through the night
(and for as long before as I can remember)
has stopped.

The Clown Painting a Self-Portrait

       *(On themes from James Ensor, particularly his mask
       paintings—"Intrigue," "The Scandalized Masks," "The
       Astonishment of the Mask Wouse," and "The Entry of
       Christ into Brussels.")*

       So James
Ensor would have seen it; slat-shanked travesty
and wry-necked twist
topped with a slack-jawed mask.

J' m' vois sitting daylong on a rusty tricycle
beside the railroad-crossing gates
trying to evolve adequate answer to the query:
"Look, kid, why

don't you go somewheres and play?"

   I see myself on a rocking-horse
all out to overtake
a cortège of broomsticks and magic carpets.
              (It was another,
              speaking in a different sort of tongue,
              who said: "I am Arnautz
              who swim against the current
              and course the hare upon an ox.")

I see myself as Buridan's ass and as a man
quite apt to happen on needles in haystacks
though with no knack for opening doors
even with the right key thrust into his hands.
   ("You try it, Sadie. We can't stand all night
   here soaking in the rain.")

   . . . or Simple Simon's pieman having missed
his only customer for all day.

   . . . Giving Delilah clippers as her Morgengabe.

   . . . And what about
the vegetarian ghoul lapping molasses
out of a saucer under the cast-iron kitchen sink?
   ("Scat! Out to the cross-roads—with your likes!"
   Bee a ell ell ess, mither. I have no likes.)

I set myself in the center
of a polygon of mirrors:
there was no reflection in any of them.

      Were you *there*—
        I mean   for Christ's
      entry into Brussels?

I was! Oh, the banners,
    Oh, the bunting,
    Oh, the bands! Oh, I,
tiered in bustle, top-hat, feather boa
and freshly furbished fleer!

The voice of the Lord spoke out of a whirlwind:
I answered Him out of a cyclone cellar.

O Caliban qui es Ariel

✻ ✻ ✻ ✻ ✻ ✻ ✻ ✻ ✻ ✻ ✻ ✻ ✻ ✻ ✻ ✻ ✻ ✻
✻   VIVE JESUS ROI DE BRUXELLES   ✻
✻ ✻ ✻ ✻ ✻ ✻ ✻ ✻ ✻ ✻ ✻ ✻ ✻ ✻ ✻ ✻ ✻

To and on Other Intellectual Poets on Reading That the U.S.A.F. Had Sent a Team of Scientists to Africa to Learn Why Giraffes Do Not Black Out

Ses ailes de géant l'empêchent de marcher.
Baudelaire

You an' me, bister, been giraffes—
equipped with them outside
terrential necks which when it comes
to trees can munch the tops of
and when it comes to telegraph lines
just snag right through them

But when it is merely a matter of browsing grass
has to can't
except they prop their
legs apart like a hasty whore
hoping to wind up work in time to catch
the 11:54
to her home in the Ramapos
or a pair of calipers attempting to describe
a circle too wide for itself to span
without spraining its furcal ligaments

And even how we keep
from blacking out
Science is still
scratching its pretty head about.

Europa

Her name
on the billboards was Señorita
Conchita de la Miranda or something of the sort
and in torero clothes with all the appropriate
skimpiness, paillettes and spangles,
she had a personable fanny and a broad
white simper to match
and a spit curl on her forehead
that looked as if
it had been painted on with Japalac.

She was supposed
to stand on a small wooden pedestal alone
in the middle of the plaza de toros
doing the living statue
and the bull, coming out of the toril,
was supposed
to take her for a real statue,
which *this* bull (hereinafter known as *he*)
possibly because he had never seen a real statue,
did not.

He came in running light and fast,
clamped to a skidding stop at the sight
of the chattering tiers of spectators
and stood a moment blinking in the sun.
Not exactly the china shop he had been
undoubtedly led to expect, but still
one does with what one has.
He lowered his head, took aim—
not at Conchita but at the pedestal
in one low-running streak.
The pedestal went skimming to the far
end of the arena and for an instant
Conchita floated in the air
like a Carpaccio angel in tight pants,
bounced once on the bull's sleek rump,
then, fast as said tight pants would let her,
scampered for the nearest burladero
with simper, spit curl, fanny still intact.

I thought of Europa and the trim
Minoan girls in their massive golden
jockstraps baiting the
black bulls of Knossos!

Noël Tragique

Tragic, said I. Oh, tragicker, says she,
than the Johnstown flood or the burning of
Washington by the British or the time
old lady Humphreys got so cruelly bit
from sitting on her upper plate that had fallen
into the bathtub, tragic as when Hera was apprised
that Zeus was two-timing her with Europa
and she, poor girl, thinking it was only a bull;
as tragic as when Deacon Fifield came to church
with his suspenders hanging and didn't know it till
he was marching up the aisle with the collection plate.

Oh, tragic, I averred, indeed. Yup, she concurred,
durn near the tragickest misfortune ever was
since the fall of the Seljuk empire . . . And a nice
girl like her, so fond
of parish activities and putting on airs!
True, we as good as knew that they were carrying on,
but you'd of thought she'd of taken the trouble to pull down
    the shade.
And right there on that fine old horsehair sofa
her great-aunt Abby left her and under that steel
engraving of poor Napoleon taking a farewell look
at his belovèd France from the deck of the *Bellerophon!*
Oh no! Oh yes indeed! You'd of thought she'd of had
more consideration. *How true!* You would have thought
she would have heard
all those carol-singers sniggering
and shoving out there in the snow. You would have thought . . .
Tragic, I call it, tragic. And all through being too lazy
to pull a shade down! Too lazy, says she,
or too much in a hurry. Or both, says I.
Or both, we both agree. Well, anyway, it's tragic.

Tragic. Tragic. Oh, woe, ah my, ah me!
And she that held her head so high, that was supposed
to play the Wise Virgin in the Christmas pageant-show . . .
The what? Haw-haw-haw-haw! Ho-ho-ho-hee!
The tragickest durn thing I ever heard!

Fragment of a Travelogue

1

Known to the vulgar—which who of us was not?—
as Li'l Booful, for short the Hydrophobia Doll
for how she had us frothing at the mouth,
for one great month she was a waitress at our mess.
It wasn't just that in those days Algiers
had fewer girls per male
than there are horned toads in the State of Maine—
oh no! that girl-child was set up
with so much the most of everything
that the morning she came to work
in a fluffy pink sweater
the young adjutant dropped a cup of
scalding coffee in his lap
and it might as well have been frostbite . . .

    Everything—and when she found herself a pair
of nylons instead of cotton ones she *had* been wearing,
a little *more* than everything
AND
those

Great Big Innocent
  (Oh, hombre, were they
      Innocent!)
EYES
     thrown in.
And when she moved about between the tables
all that
  Everything about her
             bounced:
It was like early Spring
fresh from the Forêt de Chantilly
coming around a corner at full tilt
with its arms full of daffodils.
  And when she
leaned over your shoulder
to put more butter on the table or replace
  an empty ketchup bottle,
minutes later you found yourself still
trying to eat with the wrong end of your fork.
Until one day a visiting
one-star general
took in the situation at *one* glance
and Li'l Booful at another
and the next we heard
she was up at Caserta in a sort of WAC
uniform as his non-
typing, non-English-speaking secretary.

     2
  Also there was the day
when all the Viennese
6 foot 4 of Baron von Raubitz,
knees crouched up to his ears
like an overgrown grasshopper
behind the wheel of the jeep
("In Vienna Mercedes,

Isotta, Daimler have I owned")
insisted on driving it and crashed
into a British staff car.
The British sergeant got out
and said respectfully,
   "Sir, may I see your particulars?"
"My *what?*" says Raubitz. "*What* does he want to see?"
   "Your particulars," I translated
and climbed out of the jeep and walked away.

   I never saw *him* again either
but missed him much less
than Li'l Booful,
Our Hydrophobia Doll.

The Clown as a Fox

   I have been hounded
through brush and briar and over
open rock and scree and through
swamp
and running water
and over pad-scorching sands
and nipped and harried
till of my bone and skin
no shred remains but fangs have worried,
been left no burrow
lair or cleft

I can find shelter in
no secret runway but Your guile has stopped
until of every breath I am bereft.
Where else end up my ignominious skelter
than where the bait is skewered to the tree?

Ezra Pound in Paris and Elsewhere

> ... *the loneliness of death came upon me at 3* P.M. *for
> an instant.*
>
> Ezra Pound in the *Pisan Cantos.*

1

They nudged "who's that?"
whenever in the street he,
fur-collared and no hat,
passed like a duke of Moscovy
... in the old days. . . .
head ætherial
on neck and shoulders verging burly
and profiled like a surly
somewhat older Ariel
with a streak
of Viking in him
or pre-Attic Greek,

His striking
red-gold beard and mane
curried by gales.
Whiffing centaurs' trails,

Houyhnhnm,
his gait seemed stamped with the device:
"This is not walking
This is stalking, pacing
as done by jaguar or ounce
in Zagreus' days, tracing
the lay-out for the Labyrinth . . .
   Cowflops"   (here
a flash too golden for a sneer)
"plotted Boston."

The brow bull-willed
jutting as if embossed on
Assyrian plinth
where Tiglath killed.

              2
Zagreus, they
are no maenads who gnaw thy bones to-day.
No pipes or cymbals whip a frenzy cold
as a dead snake's eye.

Orpheus, make no mistake:
   These cryptogamic bald
neuters are no bacchantes. When
these busybody scarabs have sucked their glut,
no hell would take you in.

The frowsy slut
you would have breathed
—forsooth—a soul into
has got
her teeth snagged in your jugular.
What Furies it was your delight to hatch
are now superfluous.
What perversities you cultivated

could never match
those pitted now against you.

Against such gloating odds
as these,
there *are* no gods,
sere Herakles.

                    3
And yet...
    and yet...
"So few drink of my fountain"
(although the *best* did
and came away changed men).
                    Admittedly
his true Penelope was neither Hetty Green
nor even Old Nokomis... Howlers in
eleven languages... And yet...
                    and yet...
Ecbatan to Pisa and thereafter,
il miglior fabbro...
Nothing that he ever did
or any *else* has done
has changed that
    il miglior fabbro
del parlar materno.

Postscript in Another Hand

> ... *yet say this to the Possum*
> *a bang, not a whimper*
> *with a bang, not a whimper.*
>
> Ezra Pound in the *Pisan Cantos.*

Could it be both were wrong,
Old Ez post-temporarily folding his blankets,
Mr. Eliot posteriorly acquiring pew-sheen?

   At any rate, it ended.—
Not with tea going cold in the cup
nor the smelling salts losing their savour
nor wisps
of long autumn afternoon
trailing, trailing and the smee
crying in the fog above the buoy adrift
raising suspicion that certain incantations
were losing their efficacy.

   Not this,
but not with a bang either nor even the multiple
WHAM-bangs sounding to those most concerned
like gulps of silence
(the difference needs perceiving from afar.)
Nor did the world end with God's finding a cure
for His pleonastic insomnia
nor man's
passing under an anaesthetic.

It ended with a titter, high shrill mirthless
running like flame through lint.

It ended with the atonic whinny
of the lymphatically attractive drum-majorette
being cursorily screwed under the barberry hedge blending

with the unctuous treble of the judge on the bench
ranting at manacled mutes
for the potential ambiguity of their gestures.

> (. . . *paralytic assent . . . no privacy left in any mind—*
> *no place for dove to rest a foot upon . . .*)

And after it had ended
we forgot that it had ended.

from
Asbestos Phoenix

(1968)

"*Feeling itself grow old, this bird builds itself a pyre whereon it mounts and is consumed. On the ninth day thereafter it rises from its own ashes.*"

De Algunas Bestias

Suite by the River

1   *Brittle as Threads of Glass*

                         Between
talking of kingfishers and buttercups
        (if that is what they were—it seems
        the likelier name was marsh marigolds),
we fell silent
and dabbled at the river with our toes.
            Below the bridge a pickerel splashed.
                         A dragonfly
perched
            with its angular four wings
and six abrupt
elbows   on the dry summit of a stone.
Three   four   five—
        look, there's another—minnows
wove upstream among the rushes.

    3, 4, 5 and 6 —still another made it 7—
and four wings and six elbows
and one river
and 2 people with 1 more night together . . .
It was a very arithmetical afternoon—
        brittle as threads of glass.

2   *Alba for Mélusine*

"*Et ades sera l'alba.*"

Girautz de Bornelh

Waking beside you I watch this night
dissolve inexorable into dawn.
I put words from me. No need of second sight
to scotch the lie that seas are narrow,
years short and bring no change. No,
but the hand that grips your nape
shapes its degree of meaning
and blood-beat makes this alba for our parting:

Mélusine,
     may every other man ever to hold
you cool and agile in his arms
live forever—
up to the end of time and then beyond.
Death recede from him like the lake's level
from Tantalus. Coy oblivion elude him.
Aye, more: through unabridged eternity may he
grub fallow memory fruitless to conjure up
this smooth knoll of your shoulder,
this cwm of flank, this moss-delineated quite
un-Platonic cave.

May your feet's slenderness extort of him
arid invention
without reward of recollection.
May he recall you all amiss,
     that mat black wilful mane of yours
as aureate floss, your eyes
(which are obsidian) as chalcedony.
Even may he grope in vain to find the feral low
tonalities of your unprecedented voice in darkness.

That easy puma prowl of yours
come back to him as a mere human gait,
the tanbark scent of you be in his mind
only as some vague fragrancy
of heliotrope or lilac.
                    Mélusine,
may even the name he tries to suit
his spurious evocation to
forever evade his tongue.

For that, I leave this aubade, too, unsung.

        3   *Stalled Meteor*

Stalled somewhere along its
                    give or take
          a dozen light-years
course toward Cassiopeia
    a meteor sends forth its
S O S   MAYDAY
    but in a code
so either obsolete or so not yet invented . . .

    Meanwhile galaxies
are swishing about it
                  some
buzzing it as close as
               say
n times the distance from here to Betelgeuse
      unknowing of its plight

        Stalled there as distant from
whatever there *is*
   to be distant from

          as you and I

lying in the caduceus orbit of each others' arms
impenetrably clothed in our
reciprocal nakedness

Sluiced by oncoming dawn
you are far
and near
shaped ivory whose gloss
lint of sleep a moment yet obscures

Pattern for a Brocade Shroud: After Watteau

To L. V.

1
Make it approximate:
apples and antiques,
sheen muted to an autumn-crocus tint.

The way they spoke in spirals,
sighing, "I am sew   sew . . .
we are sew   eery . . . our fingers to the bone . . ."
Slow centrifugal Norns
or call them Parcae
(depending on the climb or just the way
the ball bounces or the biscuit breaks)

Curious—
as we approached the colonnade,
this golden apple of the Hesperides

came bouncing down the marble steps and splashed
into the lagoon, frightening the swans.
        . . . We never learned: for all we know
it well may be there still.

                    Later
we strolled through stately glades
pausing to admire clear vistas
bordered, among the beeches and the yews,
by pipe-clayed clockwork statues in slow motion
of lean ithyphallic discoboli
dappled by sun and shade,
and masked diaphanous wood and water nymphs
playing the graces
with crystal wands and velvet hoops.

                2
Cut it in swaths of river mist
        Whet the scythe in early afternoon
so that the sound comes cool
and the water squelches about our ankles
        and cowbells seem
a slightly affected anachronism in the layers
of air stacked up so high behind us.

Topaz, you said the word was,
but with the swallows skimming the pool
so close their sickle wings stirred ripples,
all I could think of was obsidian

        A distinct
        tinkle breaks the "eternal silence of
        those infinite spaces."

                3
Four should be enough. If anybody asks

what we need buttons on a shroud at *all* for,
tell him it shall be answered him in time.
Let them be alternate of walrus tusk and ivory
recalling sea and sun
        awry horizons. And let the pockets be
deep and plentiful
if only to confound the adage.

        4
    Two round-trip tickets to Cythera.
There was a flinty sharpness to the wine
that was not too disagreeable: it went well
with the fake-oak paneling, electric candlesticks,
and the pigeon-eyed waitress disapproving of
our knees touching beneath the table.
                            Later,
looking up through crackled night,
we clearly heard adjacent stars
converse in muffled batsqueaks.

There was a tang of trampled leaves, a mirror
that showed us looking quite unlike ourselves
and, on the wall, a schedule of excursion trips
across the lake and a poster announcing a raffle:
        1st prize, an asbestos phoenix
        2nd prize, an adjustable Procrustean bed
        3rd prize, an imported doll made in
            Neuchâtel (Schweiz) who, when you squeezed her,
spat in your eye and enunciated, "Fuck *you*, sir!"
There were a number of other prizes:
loves, fames, fortunes—more or less helter-skelter,
as I remember—dreamless sleeps and sleepless dreams
and, for the man who thinks he has everything,
burnished steel whippets and flights
        of wrought copper birds.
The winning and the losing tickets cost the same.

5
...the cost the same...the same...
the winning and the losing cost the same
                              OMOI...
Aï de mi...The brain balks but the throat is riven.

All most a very nigh
tie weigh cup scree ming, "Home!
    O Operator, F-U-R-I 1–2
        go home."
"Go where?"
        "Please if You don't mind, home."
Comes the automated, "For that you will have to consult
your local travel agent
or the yellow pages under real estate."
    (Well, as the Swiss doll said...)

*Spoken as distinct
syllables, dully,
with no sense of
their meaning.*

        There was a fragrance of moss

                              ...grants of moss

        lichen pungency of dawn

                              ...awn

        herons standing in the fallow sedges

                              ...shallow edges

        of the lake.

Come October, great honking vees of geese
on their way south will settle here to feed.
        Winging beneath a lid of overcast,
        upward of fifty of them, so low that I could feel
        calls shaping in their throats, necks reaching,
        the pull of wing muscles. Just above
        the pasture crest, they went into
        a sudden veer, smooth, precise as if
        steered by a helm.
                              I stood there long
        among the junipers and boulders,

feeling the quiet and the chill set in.

So many speak of death who never died.
So many speak of love who know only
as much of it as lies between
thighs or books' pages.
(I speak as an old man doubting whether
he ever lived or spoke at all.)

6

"Le silence éternal de ces espaces infinis m'effraie."
Silence? M'effraie? No, I am making
no insinuations, proffering no exegesis—
merely wondering. After all, said by this
propounder of the Wager, this not unanguished founder
of the mathematical theory of probability . . .

Kids don't holler down the rain barrel any more.
It used to be a seasonable play
like spinning tops and making willow whistles.
Now, partly because there *are* no rain barrels
            (in part because it seldom ever rains),
kids have stopped doing it. I gave it up
one day when suddenly the thought
hit me, "What if this time no echo came?"
That it could never happen was reason more
for not daring to risk it.

            "My grandad always said to find live water
            it had to be witch hazel, although I've known
            some dowsers to use willow or even apple . . .

            "You know, I never really did enjoy
            church-going until I got around to being an atheist
            and old enough to dare to say so . . . Wasted years
            thinking I *had* to or leastwise *ought* to go . . ."

That was Uncle—great-grand-uncle—Simeon speaking.
He died at 96. The grandad he spoke of
could well have been alive when Watteau
was painting the *Embarcation for Cythera*.
In his last days he said, "Here I am in my dotage,
having to be spoon-fed, weaker than a babe
in body and brain, can't even pee
under my own power. I figure that if the Lord
wanted me to believe, he's big enough
to *make* me."

Not that he had ever played the fiddle much
nor well—a largo rendering of Turkey-in-the-Straw
about his limit—but that it had been *his*
ever since he swapped a dozen skunk skins for it
back in Andrew Jackson's first administration,
it was his wish to have it buried with him.
Of course he didn't get it. It would have seemed
a heathen sort of thing to do. Besides,
he'd have enough already to explain
without appearing at the Judgment Seat
with a warped fiddle he had never learned to play
tucked under his chin.

           7
Ho! Make it of—*Agitato ma non troppo*
                    . . . *non troppo*—
make it of best Jacquard brocade and chased
silver clips and clasps, the wings.
Spangle it with aglets and fourragères.
Ho! Deck it out with gold-fringed epaulets
and hashmarks from cuff to elbow.
Ho! Affix the medals, decorations, campaign ribbons,
          all three rows of them,
including Mexico (the deepest into which I got
was rigging up artillery targets in Tobyhanna, Pennsylvania)

and Salonika (the dispossessed storks
flapping above the crumpled minarets of Monastir;
the tall, black-purple, gut-shot Senegalese
glistening and grinning white with pain;
the donkey, forelegs planted wide apart,
braying back at the Austrian mountain battery).
Ho once more! the candystripe ribbon for being a volunteer
and the bronzy one with the tricolor piping—
    all of them, not excepting even
the Palmes Académiques with the rosette,
usually reserved for cuckolded
provincial music teachers.
Ho! sow the whole liberally with oak- and palm-leaf
                clusters
and, Ho! when it is finished,
present it to
      The Ishmak County Historical Museum
         —to clothe belike a taxidermic moose.

      Naked
I want to lie   naked to the
naked earth,
         on my left side
facing the point on the horizon's rim
the sun first notches at the vernal equinox.

Will I get that? Damn right I won't!
Whole sheaves of laws, rules, statutes, ordinances
stand counter to such senile whims.

Well, what about a dolmen? I'd settle for
a dolmen. No, not a phony nor even
a dismantled, reassembled one. A small
one-owner dolmen second-hand would do.
What I have in mind is something in the line
of the one I stumbled on that summer afternoon

hidden among the yellow-blossomed broom
on the downs above a loop of the Vézère.

8

Nothing to take a man up there except
an outside chance of happening upon
a tool perhaps some forbear chipped in flint
twenty milleniums ago—or utmost luck—
a bison or a reindeer he had scratched
into a patch of overhanging ledge.
(Once in an *abri* I had found a clay
loom weight astray among Solutrian celts.)

The barefoot dam in tarnished bombazeen
tending her geese beneath a fanwork vault
of chestnut trees ablaze with pollen clusters,
had warned me of the vipers. Even the poachers,
for all their leather leggings, would shun the heights
until frost came. I had shrugged her mumbling off.
But there on what could only be a dolmen's
roof or capstone, a mottled velvet coil,
slim as a willow twig, absurdly small
and frail to strike such instant awe,
raised its trim wedge-shaped head on arching neck.
Slit topaz pupils, darting tongue fixed me.

Though for the most I render gods their spite,
whatever taught that puny fellow-thing
its poise of deadly arrogance, be praised;
whatever let me never think to raise
the stick I might have killed it with, be blessed—
mean that what it may. I backed away
and watched the ribbon brightness glide between
gnarled root and riser stone.

   Afar a fox bark echoes . . .

Hawk's shadow hovers a moment on the lichened
scree . . .

9

Chorus of the Parcae (They are crying raffle tickets.
Their mist-toned chitons, voluminous and transparent,
billow in a pulsing rhythm. They speak in an implosive
whisper, subdued but, once one has heard it, compelling):
"The winning and the losing . . .
The winning and the losing . . .
Step up and get your tickets . . . tickets . . .
The winning and the losing cost the same . . ."

. . . Steel whippets
straining at their burnished fixity . . .
birds, the hammered copper birds,
congealed in flight . . .
Obsidian blade, clattering to the altar stone,
breaks with a ping like crystal . . .

Portent of autumn, a scattered burst
of raindrops sweeps
an oak-stained pool of the Vézère.

Logos

Untethered from words
Poetry could be the most—

          or better say, the only—
autonomous impulse in the world

          But then of course
there would *be* no world
          which, when you come to think of it,
might not be too great a loss.

          Imagine waking up one bright
Monday morning and—WHEE!
          Look, mom, no world!
and it isn't even monday either
          for that matter . . .

               nothing Except
one taut tenseless
               transitive Verb
          immune alike to subject and object
whose function poetry is
          to parse
throughout a pristine millenium—

          a Judgment Day
in which the whole expanding universe
is the great big bouncing Booby Prize

          till good old
(or bad old, depending on how you look at it)
Gitchi Manitou
          touches it with the business end of His cigar

               PWOP!

Shucks, don't you blubber, son. They's plenty more
where that came from.
Here, take a pocketful and blow 'em up yourself.

Unveiling a Statue
to a One-Time Poet

(*According to Lactantius, neither Apollo's flute,
Hermes' lyre, nor the song of the dying swan can
compare with the Phoenix's song.*)

In plaster effigy here stands the gawking
hero who grabbed the Phoenix with bare hands
        (Skoal, slainte, to his glory growing dim!)

Clutched by its shanks, flapping, squawking,
it battered him with wings. Its beak
jabbed out his eyes. Anus bespattered him
with noisome mutings. To the surprise
of all our clique, he held it for an instant—thus!—
quite as unmarvelous in its disarray
as bald-necked turkey or a moulting owl—
before it broke his grip and soared away.

                Through years, aging,
sightless, savaged, numb—unmanned, said some—
by the ignominious, emerald-shimmering fowl,
we used to see him groping down the street,
slavering in bistros, cadging beers,
boasting in varying versions of his feat—
claimed he had caged it, learned of it to sing
in modes too sublimate for mortal ears.
On one puke-sodden bender he even told
of roasting it: the breast, he said, was tender,
the drumstick acrid, tough,
the gizzard flecked with gold.

There came a night when we had had enough
and heaved him out. He landed on his head,
the night was cold, at closing time we found him dead.

So less in admiration than relief
and with no more remorse than is expected
of Moira's agents, no pretense of grief,
we passed the hat and had this form erected.

Dismissing bronze or marble, we chose plaster
as easier to work, less costly, crumbling faster.
For interest—since the fellow had no face
except the havoc that the Phoenix wrought,
lingam and yoni ornament the base:
they bulked so largely in his latter thought.

L'Enfance de la Sirène

> *(The juice of the wilted leaves of black nightshade is a
> lethal narcotic. Argos was Odysseus' dog, who died of
> joy on recognizing his master after twenty years ab-
> sence.)*

New canticle in mode of moss and amber—
sea wrack—
    *(bramble twitched by the sirocco
    etched the diagram on sand)*
scrived at last from the sheer headland,
emerges as first girl. Naked surprise
incised in every poise
to see her footprints patterned on the beach,
she threads through throngs of phantom lovers.
They reach to her. Not one of them perceives
she casts no shadow.

Assuming substance, they straggle back to cities
by devious routes. Later they will slake
bewilderments on trampled grass
bestrewn with cigarette butts and condoms
or on crumpled beds,
with botched facsimiles, hips creased with weals
                    of garter belts,

For no clear mountain pool
                    spilling over white pebbles,
they will wade pelvis-deep amid
water-striders and frog spawn.

The wise among them
will ask themselves no questions.
They will plug their ears with wax, lean to the oars
—yet to no homecomings.
                    The fools among them
will find native lands everywhere,
expatriate themselves from all of them.

Wherever the girl that is a canticle has passed,
they will turn up there late or soon.
Once their feet have touched the nightshade fringes
of her shadow, they will forever return
to where they have never been.

Their homecomings will be at furtive
street corners in the rain, their Penelopes
callgirls with forgotten telephone numbers.

Argos will bite them. They will be on their ways.

Homage to Paul Delvaux (1897–)

Everywhere about is landscape as far as foot can feel
lamps exude their light on flagstones
there are quaint quiet trains in
corridors of pure perspective

Out of this span of calm I rise
to hear irises unfold   moss grow infallibly
on north bark of larches   Death in temporary form
of Paul Delvaux's discreetly pubic girls
bedmates of gone goddesses walking in gardens of
undeflowered music and undeciphered roses
while waiting for their mutual dream to bring about
eclipses of the moon

I walk a long while and wait
I wait a long while and walk
I peer into a well and see a fountain
I peer into a fountain and see
the crystal chrysalis of a chaste nymph
rising toward the sliver of a moon

We load our last possessions on a raft
and hoist the makeshift sail
Our awkward innocence defies return
We know this
We feel a deep alarm but do not speak

                    Ten deliberate
adjectives too many for one volcanic
somnambulistic mound dormant but
aquiver
            fox in April in the sun

                    frisson ou pas frisson
                 frisson   frisson   pas frisson
             frisson en avril

It Happens

                                                    To M.C.

It happens
            has no name
No word stands in its path   delimits it
It happens when Goya paints
            those gloves   that pock-marked wondrous face
of the Marquesa de la Solana
When Uccello makes
            those sniggering barrel-bellied steeds
(Horse thou never wert!) and reed-like
            stands of lances
                          When Gislebertus
chisels out his Eve and Simon Magus
circa 1130 at Autun   Yes
and it happens in Stendhal's sly
            ". . . offrait à Julien   du vin du Rhin
            dans un verre vert"

In quite a different mode and vocabulary
it is what the lone
detached
            steeple at Vendôme is speaking clear
of a summer evening or a winter morning

      when there is fog and snow
It is as brightly unelaborate as Sisley's
morning of the flood at Port-Marly
or Villon's "Laissons le moustier où il est"
      or again as
chromatically positive and flat
as Picasso's brothel in Avignon

      It has little to do
      with graces and sonorities
      and is essentially incorrect
      by any standards but its own

      Such congruities as it has
      are incidental counterpoint
      of hailstones on
      slate   in zinc gutters   on lawns

It happens as
still eruption spurt
      of seed

      In instants when delight and anguish
cancel each other out in shrill conjunction
      it happens

      Girl standing by herself atop
      a stubbled hillock
      tugged at   tousled by
      November wind

Disembodied fury
crumbling geodes in its bare fists
A one-armed red   by name José Clemente
working with an absurdly small
watercolor brush on wet plaster gives us his fierce serene

Descent from the Cross
Braced   axe-wielding Christ more living
for every death He dies for us
More glorious for every degradation

            At Auvers
the red gash of road that straggled
across the wheatfield to the cemetery
has been leveled and black-topped
    the verdigris clouds and
39 crows effaced   Their flight remains

          It happens
Moan on a sweltering Brooklyn night
          (fire-escape complete with painted
                velvet cushion and transistor
"Oh, lover, hurt me hard!")
                      Rigor vitae setting in

Yes   it can happen that way too

It happens of its own
            sharp need to its own immediacy

It happens in shouts or whispers or silence
      in chords and crescendi
                  not yet set on scores
in the tread of many thousand feet
        walking in the rain

        Do not name it
It is holy   has no name

          It happens

    Not seen her

scarcely heard her name
in these near twenty years
                          I doddering when she
            was earning Girl Scout badges and
                    pigtails flying
            winning ribbons in slaloms over boys
Now she (Sister Saint Johannus in religion) learning I
(still staunch Stendhalian)
am once more scalpels' game   writes
            and says "love" 3 times on the sides
                    of a single page
and "always kept you in my special prayers"

                                    And means it
                                    And it means

It is holy   has no name
It happens
                    Do not name it

It happens in faces
            bloodied bruised by rifle butts

It happens

                    The fragile
quaintly neat spinster
            crouched in the screech of traffic
                    bleat of klaxons
cradles the ancient mongrel's grey
muzzle to her flat chest and speaks
tenderness   reassurance to his
            long deaf   now dead
ears
            half imagines
she sees his tail wag recognition

Pietà

It happens
    Oh   I too
could sometimes shout or sing or sob
    wild hosannas to Its name

Exegesis

No, lady, the foregoing poem is neither
a riddle nor a rebus. Nothing to be guessed.
When it says, "It has no name," it means just that.
No, not "grace," "vision," "caritas,"
or some exuberant, all-embracing, new,
exhilarating virtue that God and I
have just concocted.

Look, read the thing again, taking it literally.
You are handicapped by thinking of me as having
some eldritch pact with words. Whereas—
groping drop-out from night-school,
lifelong at odds with them for their chicanery and despotism—
I consort with words only from sheer loneliness,
as a lifer in solitary might welcome
the companionship of a spider or a cockroach.

                Listen . . .
No, that is asking too much. Even as I set to speak,

you gasp, "How fascinating it must be to live
in that mind of yours where everything
is glistening new and subtle and alive!
I often wonder what it must be like."

Hold tight! I am about to tell you. Mostly
it is like being a nightwatchman in a morgue
where it is always night and all of the cadavers
suffer from perpetual insomnia
even in their most excruciating nightmares,
while he himself lives in continual sick dread
of being fired.

They Danced

Off and on they danced

They danced round and round
            and up and down
They danced back and forth
            and sidewise

They danced on tiptoes and tombstones
They danced on empty stomachs and tin roofs
They danced on purpose and on a moment's notice
                on dolmens and menhirs
They danced on Saint Budóc's day
            and on Saint Cornély's

and on the Eves of Saint Winok'h
and Saint Melio, Cornish King,
On and on and on they danced

They danced to
                musettes and rebecs
They danced to large and small audiences
They danced to while away the time
They danced to and fro
They danced to jews-harps and kazoos
They danced to Jericho and back
They danced to end all dancing
They danced to rigadoons and doxologies

They danced in
They danced in couples and quadrilles
They danced in clearings and guildhalls
They danced in unison and in secret
They danced in measure
                in brains and veins
They danced in vain alas
They danced in trances and in protest
They danced in G-strings and singlets
                In spite of everything
they danced.

They danced on and on and on
and in the end
        they danced off

strewing behind them sequels
of sequins and concetti
residues of one-owner skills and skulls
and bastard urchins to boot

Laura, Age Eight

(She falls asleep across the arm of a sofa)

When this young *objet trouvé* improvises sleep
she formulates new definitions
      of grace and even comfort
as absurd
        and vice versa
as they are authentic

      Eyelashes against contour of a
cheek and nose tip
        coiled limber spine
sprawled disrupted skein of
    elbows   knees   shins
                        sneakered feet
mane whose pendant weight would be
      wasted on a pillow

This abrupt repose is of no single kingdom
      Cats and catkins have it
  colts and ferns and wild
columbine

  And in the mineral realm
some of the more improbably
      spontaneous crystals

    Patterns akin to this sometimes turn up
on beaches
      as intricately twined
roots of driftwood.

On Seeing the First Woodchuck
of the Spring
and the Last Pterodactyl

Woodchuck, if you should ask me
how one makes a poem
(stranger things than that *have* happened)
I should say
Lord, chuck, I don't know,
much the way a woodchuck
makes a burrow I imagine

You pick a likely terrain
and start digging
Follow the underground pattern in the dark
Your paws know where they are going
Don't ask them
Follow them

Make it deep enough to thwart
a poem's natural enemies
and devious enough to baffle them
Make entrances enough
to have it accessible and let the air in

Live in it a while
and alter it
shape it to your needs
After all a poem is meant to be lived in
to be gone in and out of
and to learn from

If a poet should ask me how I make a poem
I should say
I've always wondered myself.

If Ilse asked me how I make a poem
I should tell her
It is a very complicated and arcane process
In simplest analogy
it is rather like making a pterodactyl pie
First you mix your piecrust
using plenty of shortening
roll it yet keep it crisp and flaky
Then you plant an acorn
When the oak is fully grown
you lime its branches
and lie in wait for it to catch
a pterodactyl.

    Listen, Ilse,
if there is any joke in this
it is on me
on me and all the eons I've sat
beneath the oak and
even hearing the tussle and the squawks
not dared look up for fear there'd be
no pterodactyl   Yes
if I asked myself
many if not all
poems are pterodactyl pies

I could not tell this to the woodchuck
I could not tell it to a poet
Each would have his own
private dicta and terminologies
The poet comes by them by osmosis
The woodchuck has four months of hibernation
to dream them up

N.B.
  They must be real

pterodactyls.
Always one
is bound to be the last.

Keepsake

                              being at three
                                        she five
and having followed her beckon
                  through the crawl hole
           under the latticed stoop
Gerty Brukstis being so direct about it
                  (purpose mud from dust)
                                        that
even as I did not grasp it   then
                  so now
well past half a century
                  of countless confirmations
I still cannot
                  (save intellectually—and even then)
believe that it is
           that simple   *that* smoothly
                  cleft and moulded
as by a deft final swipe   of some
           unusually understanding god's
index or an angel's edgèd quill

           that easily and *that* supremely

                    good
Or that anything since Attic *lékuthoi*
could be that aptly and unobtrusively
                    designed
                                Let alone

executed.

The Neutrino
and Mr. Brinsley

> *"I think poetry should be so simple that everybody can
> understand it—just like Nature."*
> Mr. Brinsley

We poets may snatch our inspiration from mabsolutely
manything. Majestic mice, more minuscule mountains
or even miscegenate mermaids will touch us off.

Take the neutrino—of which we know the less
the more we know about it. Nevertheless
the neutrino, in a manner of speaking, *is—*
though its manner of speaking is definitely not
that of Palgrave's *Golden Treasury.*
                                You may
expound cosmology to a flower in a crannied wall,
try to convince a lark that it never was a bird.
As confidants of one's intimate frustrations,
field mice may prove as satisfactory as
psychiatrists, and they are easier to spell.

But, if you ever find yourself holding sweet converse
with a neutrino, better watch it!

       That said,
no, X does not mark the spot, because
  it isn't *there* any more
  and wasn't there in the first place—
not in any accepted sense of the word *there* ...
since, by any weekday sort of reasoning,
that which is *is*, and that which isn't,
concommitantly, is *not*. And that which, being,
in the phenomenal sense, discrete
yet has not mass, is (in this same
phenomenal sense) *not*.
      Which,
since they are traveling nonstop at some
186,000 miles a second and can penetrate
a wall of anything up to ten billion
    earth-diameters thick,
is just as well.

No, they have no electric charges and aren't
anything. Yet there are already four
known varieties of them
and probably more to come.

They are so small that the question arises
as to how and whether that which has no mass
can have relative size enough
to be smaller than something else.

It seems that near Johannesburg,
10,425 feet underground,
scientists have contrived this brobdingnagian
contraption that spatters out n billion
billions of them per second

and when, at rare intervals, ONE
    of them happens to hit something,
THAT, by golly,
      is known as a (quote) "event,"
         though to the uninitiate, one of them ever
managing *not* to hit something would seem to be a
    downright
           impossibly
             miraculous
miracle of the first water.

Yes, Mr. Brinsley, I concede the validity
of your objection that sometimes poetry is too obscure
for the average layman readily to grasp.

What was it that the man said
  about art imitating nature?

I'm not all that sure I believe it,
but there it is.

The Poet to His Mind

      My mind
at your most attractive
at those rare moments when I would not
    gladly turn you in
on an acute

case of chronic priapism   or self-replacing teeth
    you are
                 a half-grown cat   too leggy to be a kitten
    You prance arch-backed
         and pounce on unsuspecting
ideas and concepts
       clutch them with claws
             bite   rake them with both
       hind legs at once
toss them in the air   catch them   And
an instant short of boredom   conveniently contrive
to lose them   under the divan
or the radio or God
       (shall we say
            since He is not
    entirely alien to these considerations)
knows where
           Then you
lick one paw   wash the handiest
     ear and fall asleep

       Sometimes
I am not too sure that
     some of the more august among these entities
relish being cast as catnip mice.

Recital for Oboes
and a Kettledrum

        that year Judgment Day
                      fell on tuesday
—WHOOM! (muted by earthquake claps
   of bells and thunder)
Out of the dole-
fullugu-
        brious copse of woodwinds
  privately pranced a crazy
patchwork glockenspiel
   (a very Harlequin with chin whiskers and
                       chamois horns)
         slyly juggling
felt balls with his onyx hooves

   or, succubus, tinkling
her silver tits together.

Nobody saw and laughed or gasped
     or clapped his hands
     or fainted dead away or nudged his neighbor.

      What can you expect
in a world where the retina
          receives the image upside down?

    By the way,
do you know what that WHOOM this morning was?
     No, I shouldn't put it down
         to poltergeists
   nor even to termites.

       Maybe someday

when I am surer of it myself
I'll tell you

if you are still interested.

Dialogue with the Sphinx

So I spoke in a chorus of three different voices:
of a gun-shy banshee,
of a landlocked merman,
of Orpheus himself with a bad case
of laryngitis,
and said, Where is this performance getting us?

And the Sphinx—at least I took her for the Sphinx:
according to the sextant,
the fix seemed right for the road to Thebes,
and she had the same firm
hoyden impersonal breasts that Ingres
endows her with—
said, "Not much of anywhere as far as I can tell.
Where are you *trying* to get to?"
Nowhere that I know of.
"Then you are heading the wrong way,
turning your back on it. This is the road
from nowhere that you know of
to nowhere that you *don't* know of."
Is there much difference?

"How should I know? All that *I've* been to
is the nowhere that *I* know of."

So I scuffed it all out
           and started over again.

And that was that: I had spoken with the Sphinx.

Variations on a Threne
for Tristan Tzara (1896-1963)

*Tzara, gentil compagnon, sage
erstwhile infant Pope of Unreason,
in those days you decreed, "To make a poem, take
one newspaper, one pair of scissors,
snip the words one by one and put them in a bag.
Shake gently, draw them out at random,
and copy them conscientiously . . .
DADA est mort. DADA est idiot. Vive DADA!"*

Let's put them in a hat—a top hat,
a fedora, fez, sombrero, a mitre if you like.
Put them *all* in, ripe ones, green ones,
the ace of spades and a tray of diamonds,
giblets of the ram that Yahweh sent in Isaac's stead,
both ears and tail—Olé!—of Pasiphaë's bull.
Baste well with centaur's seed
and garnish with sprigs of fly agaric.

One batch makes enough for ten or a dozen servings,
depending on how hungry people are—
or spread on canapés and use for appetizers.
Some of your guests will blink and go stark mad.
Others will merely become more erotic and congenial.

Say there are eleven of them. Half are now
trussed in strait jackets, receiving shock treatment,
undergoing lobotomy. The others are
a poet, a taxi driver, his twin a
taxidermist, an admiral-of-the-fleet,
and two young virginal receptionists,
one of whom will sit beside you on the sofa,
puckering her lips and drawing what looks like
an upside down map of Florida,
explaining, "Zees ees a pootzie-ket."
(She was born and raised in Akron, Ohio.) The other
will lay her hand on the admiral's lap and ask,
"What do you *really* do when you're at sea?"
The taxi driver will be playing *morra* with the poet.
The taxidermist will be urging on the lady analyst
the advantages of mounting over cremation.

> *Tzara, even when your hair was white*
> *and you were editing Rimbaud, Corbière,*
> *propounding new interpretations of Villon,*
> *based on analyses of reams of graphs,*
> *and making do with lumpier girls*
> *than a man would by choice,*
> *I saw you still*
> *as the cherub-faced Puck with the precocious monocle,*
> *launching Dada, bubbling even then*
> *with cockeyed but genuine erudition.*

Put everything—a bit of everything,
the Holy Grail, a comet's tail, Gerard

de Nerval's pet lobster
on its blue ribbon leash—in a copper vat
or cauldron, season with a pinch of Lot's wife,
and keep it at a simmer
until the Parousia or at least until
the last disgruntled waiter starts
stacking up the chairs and flicking out
the lights.

> Tzara, I don't like your being dead.
> Somehow you seem less cut out for it
> than almost any one I ever knew.

The Magi

The three wise men looked equivocally
at three different stars.

The one who was fluent in Aramaic asked the shepherds,
"Are there in these place one inn?"

Impious shipwreck.
We had come well supplied
with slippers and sleeping pills
laxatives lighter fluid flea powder
inflatable mattresses and in case of need
a month's supply of prophylactics

Each saying, "I saw this star and
dropping everything, set out,
sur l'éperon du moment, comme disent les Anglais,
quite unprepared, just as I was."

We found three different Kristkinder
in three different mangers
and went home satisfied
leaving three different infants to make what they might
of frankincense and myrrh.

We have written three different books
all unpublished
each in his own tongue
telling of the hardships and perils of the voyage.

Street Scene: on Themes
by Edvard Munch

> *(The setting is on the Boulevard de Clichy near the gate
> of the Cemetery of Montmartre.)*

1

Don't scream.
It is only a thickset man in a dented derby
and black shoes run over at the heels. He walks
like a toy bear, its clockwork running down.
The scuffed black artificial leather briefcase
he is carrying under his arm because the rivet
that held the handle is torn loose contains

nothing but a last year's newspaper
and a package of expired foreclosal notices.

> By a blind malice, under the causeway
> of the rue Joseph de Maistre,
> is Stendhal's tomb, where a lady has just laid
> a bouquet of sea-lavender.

The girl in the faded pink brassière and panties
sitting at the fifth story window drying her hair
and believing herself invisible
is a waitress at the Dupont around the corner.
(One advantage of amnesia is the omniscience it confers.)
It is her day off—repos hebdomadaire.

Don't scream. So you do see a shoddy old archangel
with varicose veins, his atrophied, paralytic wings
concealed beneath the cape of a shabby ulster.
That is nothing to scream about. Don't look at your watch.
It is only the same time
that it was at this time yesterday.
Isn't that enough for you? . . . That is only a schnauzer
preparing to . . . Don't. Can't you see that I . . .
        I beg your pardon, was that you who screamed?

                2
No? I see . . . I see what you were thinking of . . .
This is a street scene, in a plain explicit street.
It is approximately 10:30 of a Tuesday morning,
month and year immaterial. This is the Boulevard de Clichy,
right here in Paris. It is not
the Karl-Johans-gade in Christiania.

. . . the epitaph reads: "Visse, Scrisse, Amò."
But maybe he was only boasting—except
for the writing part. Although most people have

scribbled something, not everyone has lived,
not everyone has loved. We have only
his own word for it. In any case, screaming won't . . .
In a dented derby. A schnauzer or a griffon
dubiously prospecting a last year's lamppost.
That is a waitress on her day off combing
ihr goldenes Alsatian Haar. What else
is a girl to do on her day off? Don't look at your watch.
A watched watch, sage Heraclitus says, never boils.
It is a weekday mid-morning on a busy thoroughfare.
There is traffic, autobuses, camions, taxis,
thundering in all directions.

                              The silence?
Yes, I hear it as clearly as you do,
drowning out all sound, crystalizing, crackling off
each instant into its own opaque eternity.
I hear it, but I do not think it indicates
that Judgment Day has come and passed unnoticed.
The end of the world usually makes
much more of a racket than that.

                              Look,
let's pretend that up the street under the
plane trees a squad of lead
soldiers is practicing the manual of arms. Don't . . .
Oh, all right. Go ahead. No need to fight it.
Scream as loudly as you like. I'll join you.
Both of us. Altogether now—One, Two . . .

Pardon me, do you still want to? Neither do I.

I do not think that we have met before.
No need, I think, to say our name.
Let's go and buy a sprig or two of heather
and lay it on the tomb of Henri Beyle.

Mongoose

It is not merely
that the mongoose is quicker than the cobra,
its tactics less predictable,
its counter-clockwise feints so swift
that the reptile's lunges lapse
into slow motion
nor that, putting its own
fluffed fur to fine advantage,
it is not at all impressed
by the cobra's puffed-out hood
and reads correctly
the flickering tongue as only
a measure of bewilderment.

It is not merely
that he holds the initiative
in what for him is play
that practice has made him
uncannily proficient at . . .

    His chief advantage is that
he can break the skirmish off at will,
resume whenever the fancy takes him,
always on his own terms.

    Strike or not strike,
the odds remain the same.
He can no more be parried than propitiated . . .

    though comfort may perhaps be found
in believing that he does not exist
    or is benevolent . . .
or even in the thought that,

given the initial capital and finding takers,

> we cobras could make fortunes
> by wagering against ourselves.

Some of Us
Must Remember

Some of us must remember.
(Who would have thought that any could forget?)
Some of us must remember.
We owe it to our living, to our dead,
to those who tried to cross the wheatfield
                  at Château-Thierry,
the beaches of Anzio, Tarawa, Omaha,
to those who stuck the winter out
                  at Valley Forge.
We owe it to children in playpens and in wombs.
Yes, it will whet old anguishes
but some of us *must* remember.

"Wholesale arson and murder . . .
Against the terrorism and destruction from the skies
were pitted only the courage and deep faith
of the people and their priests."
No, this is not *Pravda* nor *The Manchester Guardian*
reporting on the latest antics of Westmoreland.
(Some of us must remember—*must* remember.)

This is the good-grey, right-of-center
New York Times—April, '37: the place, remember?

GUERNICA

Shot all males above 16, shipped all the women
to extermination camps, the children
to destinations not as yet revealed,
burned and bulldozed the village to the ground.
Do you remember? June of '42:

LIDICE

Rounded up the men in barns and hosed them down
with automatic rifles. Crammed the women and children
(even the newborn are potential Communists)
into the church and gutted it with phosphorus bombs:
500 by the nearest count
of calcinated skulls. One woman crawled
through a window of the apse. A boy hid in a hedge.
Looted the village house by house before
dynamiting and firing it. Remember?
The shell still stands. June 1944: the name,

ORADOUR-SUR-GLANE

How trivial such pranks seem to us now!
PHU LY   QUANG NGAI   NAM DINH   BEN TRE
We skip the names and snicker at the quip
of Madame Nhu on "barbecued Buddhists."

Ben Tre, a pleasant city, provincial capital,
some 40,000 souls, canals bordered by evergreens and mangoes,
market center for textiles, copra, palm oil, rice.
    The bombs and shells the more effective for surprise.
Among the rubble that had been homes, shawled women
squat, rocking to and fro, and moan.
Straight-faced, an Army major explained, "It became
necessary to destroy this town to save it."
In the days when soldiers still were soldiers,

he would have achieved a twisted grin of sorts
    and set his pistol to his temple,
leaving a note requesting he be spared
burial with military honors.

Some of us must remember . . . must remember.

*Oh, who has stripped us of the sense of shame and horror
and robbed us of the precious gift of tears?*

Scherzo for a Dirge

This boy wrote . . . I don't know him, never had
heard of him . . . class of '66, dropped out
and went to help with California migrant laborers
(sounds like a do-gooder to me, one of those
potential Terroristen that the Gestapo
loved to give the works to before they turned them over—
what was left of them—to a firing squad) . . .
wrote to me enclosing a copy of the letter he had sent
returning his draft card to the local board
"as an act of total disobedience," it states.
"In the present circumstances, I must go beyond
mere pacifist, conscientious-objector, coöperation."
Goes on to quote Thoreau: "If the law
is of such a nature that it requires you
to be an agent of injustice to another,
then, I say, break the law."

"Can you," the boy asks,
"help me in this cause in any way?
Friends tell me that, noble as it may be,
what I am doing is like trying
to tunnel through a mountain with a teaspoon."

Yes, it is *that* all right. Wise friends you've got.
And no, I cannot help you, can't even pray for you.
President Johnson prays. He poses for press photographs
with bowed head, thumb holding his right eyelid shut,
auricular performing the same service for the left,
his three other fingers poised against his forehead.
It takes a very pious man to pray that fervently
with flash-light bulbs exploding all around him.

I am not that pious. When I close my eyes,
my sight turns back to Guernica, Oradour, Lidice,
Ben Tre and goes sick with shame and grief.
My only prayer would be, "Listen, Lord God of Hosts,
whatever it is that you are up to, please
lay off it, for Jesus' sake. Amen."

Maximum
Security
Ward
1964–1970

(1970)

Even the blows of heavy surf cannot cause
one sand grain to rub against another.
Rachel Carson, The Edge of the Sea

Icarus, the most eccentric [of the asteroids],
would hit the earth if its orbit changed by
only one degree, Dr. Mazursky said.
The New York Times, Oct. 18, 1967

Part One

Elegy for Mélusine from
the Intensive Care Ward

So name her Vivian. I, scarecrow Merlin—
our Broceliande this frantic bramble of
glass and plastic tubes and stainless steel—
could count off such illusions as I have
on a quarter of my thumbs.

> (. . . *even a postcard of Viollet-le-Duc's*
> *pensive chimera signed with her initial* . . .)

I penciled out a cable: FCHRISAKE COMMA
WRITE TO ME STOP YOURE LIVING AND IM DYING.
Gray lady challenged the expletive and my assurance
that it was an Ainu epithet of endearment.
I struck out everything but WRITE—cheaper
and besides I wasn't really dying
save that I couldn't breathe too well
nor feed except on intravenous dextrose.

Still stands that I am dying, Mélusine,
and have been ever since my infancy,
but the process is more measurable now.
You can tick off the months on a calendar—
eeny, meeny, miny . . . and when you get to the end . . .

> (*Today again no word.*
> *. . . Breton Saint Anne . . . Black Virgin*
> *of Le Puy* . . .)

When you get to the end . . .
when you get to the end . . .
You know what *I* should like to do when I get to the end?
when I am tucked and snug and smug
with hair combed sleek for once
pants pressed   shoes shined
and tie on straight for the first time in my life?

I'd like to give one last galvanic jerk
and flip up straight and look all living beings
in the eye—all human ones, that is
(because, less lucky than are cats and cows
and bumblebees, they know that they are living)
and speak out clear: "I hate life. I who am
no longer living can speak this truth.
From my first taste of it, from the moment when
my drunken Uncle Doc dangled me by the heels
and whacked my rump, I have always hated living!"
then flop back flat into the casket with a happy
or, at least, contented or vacuous, smirk upon my face—
soundly dead for keeps this time.
That, mes amis, would be worth living long enough to see!

      Every tear would dry like sizzled spit
testing a hot flatiron. The organ,
up to then simpering stately lullabies,
would burst a dozen pipes. The pallbearers
would stop dead in their tracks. (Their tracks to *where?*
Don't ask *me:* I'm only playing the lead
in this production, not directing it.)
And everybody from the preacher down
to the boy soprano would look each other in the eye
and murmur in unison:
"Why, the old bastard! Who'da thunk it of him!"
(It would be no time for grammatical niceties.)

Still . . .
bring on your Dead March with Muffled Drums
and Reversed Rifles and high-stepping young
Drum Majorettes with the minniest of Miniskirts.
Let Taps be played and Keeners keen.
Consume the Baked Meats with good appetite.
And . . .
grant me this: I *tried* to love life—
tried my damnedest but just couldn't make it.
Matter of acquired tastes you somehow can't acquire—
like some wines (Tokay, Monbazillac)
or foods (gazpacho, prune whip, lemon pie).

Fell fable of the fox that did at last
leap high enough and the grapes
definitely *were* sour.

(. . . *or an empty envelope addressed in her concise
swift runic hand.*)

Red-Headed Intern, Taking Notes

Do you been or did you never? Ha!
Speakless, can you flex your omohyoid
and whinny ninety-nine? Quick now,
can you recall your grandmother's maiden name
six times rapidly? Have you a phobia of spiders?
Only fairly large and brown ones

dropping from the ceiling?
Does this happen often, would you say?
(Nurse, clamp the necrometer when I say when.
If he passes out, tickle his nose with a burning feather
and tweak his ears counterclockwise.)
No history of zombi-ism in the immediate family?
And tularemia? No recent intercourse
with a rabbit?
    (Lash him firmly to the stretcher
    and store him in the ghast house for the night.)

Today Is Friday

Always it was going on
In the white hollow roar
you could hear it at a hundred paces if you listened closely
and a hemisphere away if you didn't listen at all
if you were paying no attention to it
fixing your mind hard on something else
        I will not hear it
        I will not hear it
        I

Screaming it inwardly so hard it seemed
your seminal vesicles must rupture with the strain
you could hear it close at hand
feel it crimping your nerve ends
your brain pan buckling in its grip

see it perform its curious rituals
as pale as ichor
limp as larvae
You could curl up with it and sleep
>Only it was not
>Only it was not
>Only it

You could taste it being fed intravenously through a
skein of tubes into your most plausible dreams
It was happening   It was going on as suavely
as if it were a rank of drop-forges
smashing diamonds to dust as fast as
they could be fed to them.

Tangible
It is a great protracted
totally transparent cube
with sides and angles
perceptibly contracting against
eyeballs and nose and mouth and skin

It is always happening
It is always going on
When it gets tired of going on
maybe it will stop

Via Crucis

Out of this   coming sidewise   slinking and
    sidling two steps forward and nine or ten
backward for fear of getting a charge of rock-salt
for a Peeping Tom . . . Gangway, lady! Gangway!
I'm doing a via crucis.
And she says, "B'jazes, it's the first time I ever seen
anybody doing one
in a hospital johnny! What are you—
a furriner or something?"
    Thou sayest it, lady. All these years
I've been wondering what I am and now I know:
    a foreigner or something. No kith, belike,
or kin of anything—at least among the higher primates—
a, biologically speaking, sport!

By what, for all its blare, must still be night,
the swift square-bottomed nurse flits sure
from bed to bed, takes blood pressures and pulses,
checks drains and bandages, switches on chest pumps.
Interns, doctors, moving in pairs,
converse in muffled nods. Approaching with a clipboard,
a small wren-faced nurse asks, "Sir,
what is your religion?" Religion?
"I have to ask you just in case." None.
She marks the X at Protestant.

MR. GOLDBLATT: STAFF NURSE (white letters on
blue plastic badge) buzzing like an officious
bottlefly doing an imitation of Schnozzle Durante,
struts in by what, if they would give me back my watch,
must now be morning. There are no windows though
to judge that by, only these cones of light
trained on our eyelids . . . high iron grills

fencing in each of the nearly touching beds
constantly being (one man dying or making guggling
sounds of death, another in new-bloodied bandages
arriving) trundled in or out.

    "HELLO, OL' SPORT! How you doin', ol' sport?
Come on, ol' sport, roll over so I can insert . . .
Look here, ol' sport, you just always do
just like I tell you and we'll get along fine."

Maximum Security Ward. Sure, I know . . .
Intensive Care Ward, but none the less,
straight out of Jacques Callot by Hogarth.
    "What time they bring him in here? 2 a.m.?"

No, so to speak, white corpuscles. Your guess
why not, as good as mine: all I know
is chattering teeth and thirst.

    "Look here, ol' sport,
I give you ginger ale a while ago.
You'da been thirsty, you'da drunk it
instead of yammerin' for water now.
You don't like ginger ale, it ain't my fault.
I'm busy now, I got my records to keep up."

MR. GOLDBLATT, you cloacal breathed, glad-handing ghoul,
if ever I get my white
corpuscles out of hock
and temperature down enough to take it orally,
I'm going to vault that side rail and ram
those outsized, clicking dentures down your throat,
God be my witness. SELAH.

Cadenza

"My name is Marsyas,"
                    says ram
says ram to Abraham
caught in the thicket by the horns,
"My name is Marsyas."
Name of father? "None.
Look, I know an altar when I see one."
Name of mother? Come on, name of mother?
"All right. Hagar.
And don't make believe you never heard of her."

The square-bottomed nurse's night is over.
She is about to leave. She wipes
sweat from her forehead
and pushes her hair back under her cap.
She stops, turns back. "You comf'table? You don't look it.
You want I should see if I could do
sumpen about those pillows before I go?"

Scene: A Bedside
in the Witches' Kitchen

DOCTOR *to his retinue of interns and residents:*
    Obvious ptoritus of the drabia.
    Although the prizzle presents no sign of rabies,

note this pang in the upper diaphrosis.
When kicked there hard enough, the patient utters,
"Yoof!" and curls up like a cutworm.
I prescribe bedcheck every hour on the hour
with intensive catalepsis. (*Exeunt.*)

PATIENT *to Nurse:*
My name is Marsyas, a stranger here.
                How to explain?
Sprächen zoo something? anything? Aard-vark? Gnu?
you look well-meaning. If I made noises in my phlarynx
and shaped them with my phtongue, would they have
snignifigance to you? Or would they merely
confuse us further? Let's go about it anagogically.
Close your ears. Go twine your sphygmomanometer
about some other patient or administer him his hemlock,
while I supplicate.

            Today is Friday.

Gamut of goddesses, Gaia, Latona, Frigg whose day it is,
cat-flanked Ishtar with the up-turned palms,
Rosmertha of the Gauls, with grief-gouged eyes
and rough-hewn cleft—
            sister, mother, mistress of the dead,
mare-shaped Epona, you, Venus of Lespugue
in mammoth tusk, majestic at scarce a handsbreadth tall,
though not quite small enough to put into a matchbox
and walk the streets of Montparnasse with in your pocket . . .

Gamut of goddesses,
in your spare moments intercede for me . . .
      (Breath comes scant now,
        but by chance you may have heard,
            my name is Marsyas) . . .
intercede for me. Let me be never born.

Let my ghost wander in brambled upland meadows.
Drizzle in evening streets, may she at times recall
our walking there, arms pressed to ribs together.

Mélusine!

Montparnasse . . .

Montparnasse
that I shall never see again, the Montparnasse
of Joyce and Pound, Stein, Stella Bowen,
little Zadkine, Giacometti . . . all gone in any case,
and would I might have died, been buried there.

[GIACOMETTI]

". . . impression that art would come easy to me . . .
getting what I wanted . . . now, 50 years later . . .
At 13 I did a head of Diego and have done
nothing better since . . . Am no closer.
Tintoretto effaced by the Giottos of Padua
blotted out in turn by Cimabue . . .
Sculpture anti-form—*of*, not *in*, space
. . . rather see a bird flying in the sky
than any masterpiece of art . . ."

A fixture in the quarter with his furrowed face
from the first day he came there
to study with Bourdelle.
Giacometti standing in the dank, littered shed

that was his atelier, lighting one Gauloise from
the short stub of another, standing because
there was no place to sit, explained
a great many things, such as carrying about
his work of four whole years in half-a-dozen
matchboxes scattered through his pockets and working
for years with the same model without ever
speaking to her—explained many things by saying,
"La vie n'est qu'un suicide passif."
That's one way of looking at it; it takes longer
than holding your head in a gas oven
or jumping off the Pont Neuf some darkish night,
but just as effective. He proved it: lung cancer, 1966.

Gamut of goddesses, intercede (presumably with
yourselves) for me.
                    Today is Friday . . .
                                    vendredi . . .

Venus of flesh . . .
              (Landing at Naples:
      Colonel Bill's curly-headed
      unpanted daughter panting for the plane.)
Au fond perhaps   of limited lascivity . . .
Les yeux cernés, tendres mais sans la moindre tendresse.

"Side by Side"

Side by side   but scant sharing
Little of fellowship here   Some of us for dying
      Some for living   Some half a mind each way.

      Should I have willed my corneas?
      My old but still staunch heart?
      my cadaver *in toto?* Medical schools will pay
      good money in advance for a second-hand cadaver.

            No! not to have my brine-shriveled scrotum
      bandied about, my epididymis unraveled, measured by
      some embryo Bovary.

No fellowship . . . How the dying wince
            from the living's shadows!
How the living fear the kinship of the dead!
I do not know which side I'm on—
the dyings' or the livings' (that small minority,
of us though not aware of it)
No, on the whole, I am on the side of the dead once they
   have
achieved atonement with the earth
and of the living who do not want
even in their secret hearts to die.

      "I don' wanna by-nit up me arsole
      I don' wan' me bollicks shot awy-y-y
      I wanna go to Blighty
      To dear ol' blinkin' Blighty
      An' there I wanna fook meself awy-y-y."

Singing this or something similar with gusto
as they trudged up into the lines at 2nd Mons,

humming it under their breaths, wriggling on hips and elbows
across no-man's-land between the bursts of starshells.

> "Leaned on the trigger and let the blighter 'ave
> a bellyful just as 'e was abaht
> to let *me* 'ave a 'titer-marsher—
> narsty fings them 'titer-marshers.
> Don't harf mike a mess of yer, they don't."

> *I wanna go to Blighty*
> *To dear ol' blinkin' Blighty*
> *An' there I wanna . . .*

"Got it proper, ol' Robby did. Real cushy.
Though Ah donno's Ah'd want it that bad—
as soon they didn't ship me home. Just
patch me up an' shove me back into the trenches.
Don't need 'em none for fightin'.
Maybe 'appier without 'em anywhere, but still an' all . . .
Goin' down from the dressin' station,
all bandaged so you couldn't reely tell,
wot with all that dope shot into 'im,
but kinder guessin', he says, 'Sy, mitey,
'ow's for the loan of your Enfield for a sec—
just to kinder finish up the job?' "

A coward dies a thousand deaths.
Rate me no coward then: 990-some yet to go.
Just seven as I make it, three times with pneumonia
(out of ten in all). Once Naples to Algiers
flying the deck—that hungry waterspout.
The kiefed-up sidi with the razor in the tram.
Once coming out of anesthesia with
an oxygen mask and much undue ado.
Then this last time, so close they thought it best
to take the copyright in my wife's name.

        Don't count
that afternoon at Flirey: handful of us standing around
watching a chess game under an oak
and desultory one-o-fives looping overhead
and landing in the beet fields half a mile beyond . . .
If you hear it, it is not for *you*. Look hard
and you could even see them, bumbling lumps
with the muzzle velocity of an oxcart.
The zouave had just castled and announced,
"Echec au roi."
Wordless, triggered by a sudden hunch, we flowed
down into the dugout.
The zouave—he owned the game—it seems reached back
to snatch the white queen, his *porte-bonheur*.
We heard one WHUNGPH, waited a moment to see
if there were more to come, decided not,
emerged in time to see the *brancardiers*
loading the zouave's remains.
As Louis told the tale, his hand still clutched
the lucky queen and the *obus* had landed
in the exact center of the chessboard—
accurate within perhaps ten paces.

I do not count that afternoon nor would
if the fuse itself had struck
square on my cranial suture, death no more
real for me than for the fool squirrel
racing to throw a body block
on an oncoming truck.
        Too young to think that we could ever die.

The Cube as a Wilted Prism

The
walls now extend   recede to everywhere.
The ceiling, though still low, outcrops the stratosphere.
The drop-forge rank
chumbles and crunks more diamonds faster into dust
and grids space with crisscross false horizons.
Distance presses, cramps, distends.

This cube
has 6 faces, 12 edges, 24 angles
each more fluctuating pinched and forced a-spread
than all the others. Space. Sculpture not *in*
but *of* Space. Eroding Space. Ripples,
billows, bellies out to burst,
yet, contracting, shrinks tight within, upon itself—
soundless explosion squeezed to utmost condensation.

    (I *know*—like trying to explain
    the concept and sensation of
    wetness to a, say, intelligent and
    articulate fish, *piscis sapiens*—
    or darkness to a mole.)

. . . become a fast-expanding, prismic,
limp though hard, Brobdingnagian HERE including THERE,
devoid of direction.
You might scream now if you so wished:
sound cannot travel in such vast whiteness.

Equation with death—liquescent crystal Death,
as dry, invisible as pure
self-consuming flame,
becomes inevitable.

The cross-hair sight of Never and Now
is set in all zeniths, on all horizons.
It is stamped with hot wire
on my breastbone.

Polar Bear

That time coming out from under
sodium pentathol my first words were,
"I dreamt I was a polar bear
that couldn't write poetry."
Literally but to unhearing ears.

    Adrift upon that slab of floe
    under a slate sky
    his conic white
    snout swaying in unison
    with words that never came.

The small deft nurse who held
the glass tube to my lips
said, "Sip slowly,
a little at a time. Don't raise your head."

I, not yet aware that words were speech,
informed her,
"You are quite lovely
with your copper hair.

You look like something that was turned
          into a flower
before it was a girl again . . . I can't explain."

Later she came back and asked
how I was feeling. "Not bad," I lied,
the anesthesia now wearing thin.
She laid her hand against my face.
"Still you had better have this though."
An easy needle slipped into my shoulder.

A polar bear who could not . . .
Rocking his baffled muzzle to and fro
groping for the tempo of a world
empty of both sense and sound.

I wondered—whatever was in the needle
taking now effect—what had become of him
and brooded over not trying to find a way to help him,
staying at least to share
the anguish of his white bewilderment.

The Archangel Michael,
or a reasonable facsimile thereof,
holds a press conference:

". . . Embarked upon a Holy Crusade whose
holy purpose . . . on this there is no general accord."
[Subdued applause.] As Mr. Eisenhower has explained,

'the natives were tired of *any* form
of overlordship . . . wanted their independence'
and having won it, took it into their thick peasant heads
to resent the mercenaries whom we sent
to liberate them from it—
instead of turning the other cheek to be kicked.

"Holy—as I was saying—Crusade.
What them native races need is a little humility,
start off by getting right down on their knees
and praying the good Lord to give it to them.
What you mean—the Buddhists *have* no god?
Don't they worship idols or something
like everybody else? Maybe that's right where
the whole trouble lies!"

> "*. . . All because we do not car-ry
> Everything to God in prayer.*"

"Yessiree! You just try that next time
and see if everything won't come out right.
That way, about the only trouble that a fellow
can have is getting callouses on his knees!"

ME, MEL TROTTER, LORD,
You remember? You found me lying filthy drunk
in a gutter, Lord, so hog-dirty no human being
would have wanted to soil his hands by touching me.
But You did, Lord.
You picked me up and washed me in Your own Son's blood
and sent me forth to preach Your word throughout
the length and breadth of this whole land.
What did I ever do to deserve it, Lord?
Nothing, O Lord. Nothing.
All I deserved was hell-fire, but You had mercy on me.
You and Your Son. You sent me here tonight, Lord,

to pass Your holy Word on to these boys.
They too are sinners, Lord, but that won't keep You
from entering right into their hearts and making them
clean and pure   Let us now sing together:

> *Just as I am without one plea*
> *But that Thy blood was shed for me*
> *And that Thou bidst me come to Thee-ee,*
> *O Lamb of God, I come, I come.*

Will you come to Jesus? Will you let
Jesus come into your heart? Will *you?* Will *you?*
Hold up your hands, brothers, if you will.
Will you give yourself to Christ? Hold up your hand . . .
I see you, brother . . . I see you, brother . . . I see you.
And what about *you*, brother? Are you too *brave* to come
to Jesus? Too sure that you can face temptation all alone?
So certain that you can lick the Devil singlehanded
that you don't *want* Jesus on your side? We're waiting,
brother. We're praying for you.

> *Just as I am and waiting not*
> *To rid my soul of one dark blot*
> *To thee, whose blood can cleanse each spot,*
> *O Lamb of God, I come, I come.*

AN USHER (*whispering loudly. He is also co-captain of the*
football team):
Come on, guy. Put up your hand
We want to make this school 100% for Jesus Christ.
Put it up. Do you want him to keep us here all night?

> *Holy, holy, holy . . .*

The press conference ends when the sergeants-at-arms,
preceded by a huge bass drum, march in singing,

"*Onward Christian soldiers, marching as to war,*"
and carrying pikes on which heathen heads with
wispy beards are impaled.

Inventory

      Hmm, let's see now . . .
On the left we have what is left
On the right is what is right
It is that simple . . .
   Faith, hope and clarity . . .
I knew a girl named Faith once,
on shipboard and in both senses

     To be a model patient you lie on your back,
     screen your eyes with the back of your wrist
     against the glaring cone of light
     and wait the chance to pour unnoticed
     the ginger ale into the urinal—
     bringing variety into the life
     of some laboratory technician.

Gamut of goddesses . . . with a few gods thrown in . . .
Diana of Ephesus with her cluster
of breasts, looking like something dreamt
of a Saturday night by a perverse computer
primed with LSD . . .
Priapic Marsyas or Silenus as shown

on a black-figured vase ("young man from Nantucket")
tootling his heart out
on upraised double flute . . .

Check again, placing the patient this time
on a sphere spinning on its own axis at
1000 miles an hour and in its orbit at
66,000 mph. And now?
                    Through dizzy eyes:
On the left is nothing left
On the right nothing is right.

I have lived. Listen to that!
Say it again, ol' sport. *I have lived.*
            Of all the witless things to say,
I give you this!

Gamut of goddesses, Nerthus, Frigg (Friday's girl),
Rosmertha and You
the veiled and nameless one, bless me.
Still the blood-flow in my veins,
numb fingers' touch, quell thought and feeling
in my brain.
            For now,
surveying that churned wake, I know
that by some slip or quirk,
I have led a stranger's life, known with his mind,
spoken with his tongue, kissed with his lips,
worshipped or denied his gods . . .
    (Mix-up in cloak-room checks—
            sole-print perhaps)
and now must die this death of his for him.

The Flute

MARSYAS: (*He takes his flute and seems about to play it, thinks better of it and slips it back into the pocket of his bathrobe. He resumes his meditation.*)

'A stranger's life?' I said. *Many* strangers.
Known with their minds . . . their eyes . . . their lips . . .
Worshipped their gods . . . heard with their ears?
Felt, have I, with their hearts—a moment mine?

    That appeal—in Mozart now, I mean, the string quintet.
Adagio. Muted—you can't mute a flute.
Two notes legato: *sol fa.* A silence.
    Two notes: *do si.* A pause buoyed up and weighted
        with grief too pure to *be* grief—
or any other feeling *I* could ever know,
and then that linked descending run . . .
        The ache and wonder!
And *simple.* Two notes. A rest. Two more notes,
higher this time—appealing, questioning, calling out—
        to what?
A rest. And then that flow.
That's all that I remember clearly of it.
    (*He takes the flute again, looks at it dubiously, puts it to his lips and plays:*

He listens for a moment, takes the flute between his hands, breaks it in two and drops the pieces to the floor. The night nurse picks them up and hands them to him. Without looking at her, he carefully puts them back into his pocket.*)

Icarus Agonistes

A damsel with a clip-board in an Intensive Care Ward
once I saw
in a white uniform and she was asking,
"Sir, what is your religion?" with a pencil poised
to check it off. I should have said Black Muslim,
but I didn't think of it until a week later.

　　. . . one straggling and on the whole
　　incurious sheep that happens
　　to be facing the other way from
　　the rest of the flock seems to have heard the splash
　　and paused an instant in its cropping . . .
　　the shepherd gawking but in the diametrically
　　wrong direction.

　　"Come on, ol' sport . . . ol' sport."

Stand on a haystack and flap your arms.
You see, you almost *did* fly! Someday
try it from the corncrib roof. Or, Joshua—
hold up your arm and, as watching your shadow
you can clearly see, stop the sun for a split second.

　　C'est pourtant vrai: Mourir c'est partir un peu.
　　(Sure, I know how it *should* go. If I don't think
　　hard enough about it, I know how almost *ev-*
　　erything should go. The trouble is
　　sometimes I think, and I'm not good at it.
　　Right now I think I hear a tinkling sound
　　above all other racket. And *mourir* is
　　partir quite a lot.)

I see a cart.
Please, Mr. Good Humor Man, you with the starched
white clothes! (I see the cart and hear the jingle.)
Would any of your tranquilizers lay
the ghosts of Twink and Stella? Norman Fitts?
Please, Mister Good Humor Man, You with the long white
   beard
and cart and bell. You, Mister Summertime Saint Nick,
I have died my allotted thousand deaths
and served my time in hell
after each one of them.
               The bell, please. The bell . . .
You may not have noticed it, but I've been out on my feet
since the first round. Really *out*,
slobbering, glassy-eyed, rubber-legged,
hooking my chin on something's shoulder and hanging on
to hear the bell

      The winnuh
            and still champeen
   is whatever
         I got myself overmatched with
     from the start.

(From somewhere a very old and tired tape
   is heard faintly urging:
     "Fight your *left*, baby! Fight your *left!*
Back him up, baby! Back him up!
Fight your left! F'get yuh got a right! Don't think,
just fight your left!"
         BONG.
"Listen, baby. Can yuh hear me? Yuh still got him cold
if yuh don't go right-hand crazy. Fight your left.
Don't think. F'get yuh *got* a brain."
         BONG.
"Awright, baby. We get him nex' time maybe.

Him or somebody else.
                    Plenty times already
you been flattened almost as bad as this.")

Fiercer Than Evening Wolves . . .

Lying here in truth more disgruntled
than in any great discomfort, shaped to this
tapered wedge of cosmos, wondering
if there would be relief in having a God to hate . . .
I've tried it—believing there was one, that is.
"Everything," says Blake, "possible to be believed
is an image of the truth." Whether a God's being
is "possible to be believed" by me
I shall probably die without discovering.

To while the night away, try now imagining
for symbol's sake a man bigger than
any professional basketball or football player.
Something to the scale of the Rhodes Colossus
or the Pharaohs of Abu-Simbel. Bearded. Naked
or in a sort of off-the-shoulder toga? Both.
And with a clutch of writhing thunderbolts.
Zeus, Thor, Quetzalcoatl all in one.
Endow him with omnipotence, omniscience, omnipresence . . .
All to no end.

    I lie here remembering, half-envying
my truly pious mother, who did believe—

totally, always, absolutely and without
shading or limitation   and died
selecting, as she hoped,
the most telling of blasphemies,
mastered her mangled speech to utter it precisely,
enunciated, "God is a cunt," straining to say
the word for the first time in her life,
sure that He was hearing her,
that she was in His hands
and soon would stand defenseless
in His presence.

"What," the red-headed intern asks, "did your father die of?"
Another's suicide. Illuminating gas. He broke down
the door of the hotel room. The blast
broke windows blocks away.
"And your mother? Please, no accidents."
This was no accident. Of that we can be sure.
Swallowing a massive dose of potassium chlorate—
no, not the cyanide she'd begged me for—
in the charity ward of the New Haven Hospital.
The story, both longer and shorter than it should have been,
boils down mostly to arithmetic? How is
your arithmetic, doctor?

THE ARITHMETIC LESSON

If one room's rent with cooking privileges came
to $7 a week, and 60 times 20 cents an hour
is $12 and you had to put a quarter in
the gas meter from time to time and shoes
and clothes wore out or got outgrown and on
days when you were working on the other side of town
you had to take the trolley,
how did you eat and feed your young?
Simple. By taking in sewing to do at home
nights and Sundays. Quod erat demonstrandum.

Evenings between
cooking and doing the housework and getting back
to sewing, she would read the Bible to me.
Especially the Old Testament. I liked that best—
even Jeremiah and Habakkuk . . . *Their horses swifter*
   than leopards and fiercer than evening
      wolves . . .
and Ezekiel with his cherubim on beryl monocycles.
She skipped the parts about Dinah's boy-friend
getting circumcised and the two Tamars
and the Lord making the Israelites
hamstring the horses and rip up
the bellies of pregnant ladies.
Yes, the Lord God fared very well by Her—
better than She did by him, by far.

In her mid-forties when successive strokes
twisted her mouth awry, mangled her speech,
paralyzed the right side of her body,
there were, each with its acute
eternity enhanced by helplessness,
some 86 thousand seconds in a day.
"She's young," the trim-cut doctor jibed. "May well
live on like this another twenty years."
Roughly 600 million seconds, each more
desperate than the last.
         Would you let
a half-crushed spider live a millionth part as long?
      ". . . fiercer than evening wolves . . ."
   Does that answer your question, doctor?
   Nothing hereditary, I should say.

The Oracles

```
            HAPPEN
        OR DO NOT HAPPEN
     HAS OR HAS NOT HAPPENED
     WILL OR WILL NOT HAPPEN
```

gouged on a crude lead slab set into
the most remote blind gut of the cavern.
Mephitic vapors will extinguish torches.
It can be deciphered only by touch.

Hugging her breasts, the Pythoness rocks in anguish.
Deep in her trance, she sees with open eyes
all that has been and is about to be.
Hugs her breasts, rocks to and fro and moans.
She wakes. Juice of freshly pressed nepenthes
dribbles from her slack mouth.
The wail becomes a whimper, a gape, a blank
foolish, rather evil, smile.
                            She knows
and cannot undo knowing
        nor forget she knows.
        Her eyeteeth are small fangs.

She cannot weep or pray:
all that has ever happened
        all that is to happen
she knows.

There Are Those

Qui bien ce croit, peu ne merit
Gens mors estre faiz petiz dieux
François Villon

There are those—with mine own eyes I've seen them,
heard them with my own ears—
who still contrive to believe in heaven,
locus undisclosed, though rather up than down.
(Quoting sound authority, "All men will arise
with the same bodies they have now." Is that
something to feel good about?)

Alice B. Toklas, passing from Jew to atheist to
Roman Catholic, on being baptized, asked,
"Does this mean I'll see Gertrude when I die?"

Our belovèd Walshes—Paddy and Mim!
Come straight from Dublin to Arizona, himself
having but half a lung (T.B. arrested when we met them).
The warmth and wit of them. The good foolish
games that we concocted. The good talk.
The punning Latin sonnets to wish us happy birthdays.

"Look, Paddy, nothing could ever make me believe
in that heaven of yours."
"Of God's, more strictly speaking . . .
And all the luckier for you. Think of your surprise
when you'll be waking up and saying, 'I still don't believe
in all this heaven stuff!' and God just grinning,
'Nor do you have to, man. Not if not believing
makes you any happier. We aim to please.' "
"But if there were a heaven, what makes you think
I'd ever get there?"
"Because it wouldn't *be* a heaven

for Mim and me unless you were." And Mim,
though apt to leave theology to Paddy, joined in,
"That's God's own truth—it wouldn't be, you know.
But you'll be there all right. We being older,
we're like to get there first. You'll find us waiting."

Paddy . . . Mim . . .
I hadn't seen you all these forty years.
Two Christmases ago we didn't get
our usual letter from you.
Later a stranger wrote that you had died
a week apart, leaving word that you had always missed us
and never known anyone you'd been fonder of . . .
    Paddy . . . Mim . . .

Paddy was a man—a good man but still
    only a man.
If I know Mim, it would take a lot more
than there not *being* any heaven
to keep her from going there, if only to make sure
that Paddy had all he'd ever need to make him happy—
Not but what she trusted God . . .
        but still . . .

The Prayers

To M. C.

Prayers, I age 8 asked, do they get answered?
The reply was patient but categoric.
Then why not, instead of asking for just enough

to make some payment on back rent, pray big—
ask for a hundred or a billion dollars
and never have to bother Him again?

Interrogatory prayer, whom are you asking what?
"I'm asking the dead what death is like and the living
what it is like to live. I am asking this housefly,
sealed somehow between panes, perhaps hatched there,
buzzing its life away against impenetrable light,
whether it would rather be let out into
the foreign air, stay where it is, or be
let in and whacked by a flyswatter."

Look, fly. I won't hurt you. I only want to scare you out.
Don't waste your life penned up in here
where there isn't any future for you.
Don't you want to copulate and eat and see
                    something of the world?
I'm unfastening the storm window for you.
Get the hell outdoors where you were meant to be.
Nothing was ever meant to live in houses.
Doesn't it give you claustrophobia? It does me.
Even *cimex lectularius*, more familiarly known as bedbug,
's natural habitat is outdoors under the bark of trees.
In the beginning *was* no bed (see
Genesis 1:1–2, St. John 1:1, and Faust's
'Im Anfang war die Tat'—Deed, indeed!)
Adam begot Cain, Cain begot Enoch . . . Lamech begot
Jubal, father of all flute *and* harp players.
And Abraham upon Hagar, his maidservant, begot
Ishmael whose 'hand will be against every man,'
—all at least 34 hundred years before
the first inner-spring mattress was invented.

Gamut of goddesses, Eastre,
Black Virgin of Le Puy,

Louise Michel, *la vierge rouge,*
born to a maidservant by the master's son . . .
last stand of the Commune, surrounded, hopelessly out-armed,
   outnumbered,
in the Montmartre cemetery—
about 30,000 murdered out of hand,
the survivors, she miraculously among them,
deported half-a-world away to New Caledonia.
Came back to preach LIBERTY through France
unto the day she died.

"My name is Marsyas,"
        says ram to Abraham.
"I play the flute. Keep your rabbinical hands off me.
I know an altar when I see one.
And no good ever came of one yet.
By the way, where is your *real* firstborn,
the one you drove into the desert?"

Hey,
interrogatory prayer! I'm not done with you yet.
Whom else do you ask what else of?
"I ask all sorts of things all sorts of questions.
I am asking questions of the walls and ceiling,
of the cocoon of bandages in a coma beside me.
I am asking questions of the ground and sky
of places I shall never see again, asking our belovèd
Mim and Paddy Walsh if there really is
a heaven (they owe me a jug of corn whiskey if there isn't)
and how they like it there.
I am asking the handsome Black Muslim masseuse
on 88th Street, who told me, 'I jes' *love* po'try!'
whether she ever spreads her fine, strong,
horse-chestnut-textured legs to Allah.
I am asking questions of skin and nerves and glands,
tits and tummies. I am asking lips
how they first learned to suck, to shape first words.

Here I am, not too short of being dead
and with no idea of what one actually *does*
to perform such simple acts as swallowing and sneezing,
let alone ejaculating or falling asleep."

(*You, Ishmael, take Marsyas, to be your blood-
brother. Make your X there in the lower corner
and don't read the fine print too carefully.*)

Exploratory prayer, addressed to whom?
what are you asking It or Her or Him
to say or do? What language, spoken by what
paralyzed or petrified tongue, are you uttered in?

Formed not of dust but quicksand.
Lie prostrate in the muck, face buried deep in it,
and try
for breath to
propitiate
Him, Her, or It
with gasping mad doxologies and screamed hosannahs.
          . . . and yet
. . . and yet
               . . . ram caught by the horns
               in a thicket. We find the theme
                    in gold and lapis lazuli at Ur of the Chaldees.
          Poor bloody Marsyas—teach him to steer clear
                         of angels
("A little lower than the angels" . . . ,
Some of whom
          could walk under a snake's ass
with high hats on . . . unquote the sergeant
          who had served in the calvary
          with Captain Black-Jack Perishing
          christianizing them Moros in the Philippines)
and yet
               . . . And yet . . .

"Loin de Moi . . ."

Robert Desnos

Far from me
light shattering copper balls across
the stubbled hillsides in October
seeing fox pounce daintily on crickets,
standing on a boulder acknowledging
the reverent ranks of mullein,
flapping my wings and disclaiming, "No.
I am not God! I am not God! . . . Only
one of his archangels, Michael for choice,
excepting on such days as I fill in
for Israfel or Orpheus."
Far from me godhood
and the creaking crazy stars doing
their cumbersome quadrilles to patchwork patterns
concocted here on earth: Bootes the Herdsman,
Lyra and the ram Aries.
Far from me vermeil diadem, globe and scepter,
loving-cups for taking Beelzebub in straight sets
or scoring eagles over Satan. Far from me be
all honors, loves and worships except a few
passing and very momentary idolatries.
Far from me in this moment
everything that lived and now is dead,
everything that lives and soon will die,
everything I loved that now is gone.
You who were absent from the place of the Skull,
let my self itself be far from me.
Far from me. Far from me. There is no return from here
to color, clarity, or form. Sound aplenty
but not a thud or scrape or drone to shape to any harmony.
There is a stocky, squat, somebody's sister—
somebody's daughter, at any rate—with swollen ankles,
blouse like saddlebags. Night built up in layers

of chlorine and last year's puke and piss.
If I should beat my head against the bars,
they would put it down to delirium.

Dawn . . . dear Mr. white-jacketed God, please send dawn.
Dawn. I couldn't see it here
but maybe catch a whiff of it.
I am stretched out here dreading dawn as if it were
a more malignant form of night.
(I must not let myself guess that.)
I am lying here trying to remember how to laugh
against the chance
of anything to laugh for   ever again occurring.
I am lying here not screaming—as good a pastime
as any. I am lying here trying to refrain
from trying to remember anything.
I am lying here stifling in the rutty goat smell
of MR. GOLDBLATT:STAFF NURSE and death.

Mélusine!
("I cannot write," she said. "For me a letter
is artifice that only enhances distance and
aggravates the ache of separation." Clasping my hand
beneath a café table at Montparnasse.)

I am lying here trying not to see these bars,
not to envy everyone who died with pants on—
those, for instance, who went down in flames at La Chaussée.
Lying here wondering what I am doing here at all.
No. I don't mean here in this death house.
I mean HERE where MR. GOLDBLATTS are.
I mean here in these United States— "Breathes there
                a man with soul so dead . . . ?" Yes, I do—
though for how long I cannot say.
I mean this world, for that matter, this human world.

(I never asked to be human. I don't and never did
opt to be human. Given any choice, I should rather
have been begotten by a dog-fox on a vixen
or an alley tom on a good mouser or—
though that may be too much to wish—
not to have been begotten at all. Quarter of a billion
spermatozoa scatter-sprayed, one gets its random target,
to the ultimate consternation of all concerned.

I never wanted to be *me*, in this at least
I found, it seems, fulfillment. (Listen carefully, cat,
cock your head on one side and wrap your tail
about your paws. You stand as good a chance
of understanding this as any.) I cannot think
of anyone less me than I am. There should be
surcease in that. Everybody—the red-headed intern,
the old man making death-sounds in the corner crib,
the low-slung nurse winding up her nightly stint . . .
Even the CHIEF HEAD IMPERIAL MR GOLDBALLS: STAFF NURSE
is more like me than I am.

. . . sizzle out like crackerbarrelers' spit
on the potbellied stove . . . sizzled out . . .
like other lives . . . What kind of a life is that,
a life like other lives, I ask you?
                              No,
I don't ask anybody anything. Not even what
time it is. Not even anything. Just as I wouldn't—
after the Sopwith fell apart and bent
the machine-gun yoke across my forehead
and Raz came down a few days later
to see me at the hospital—I wouldn't ask the bastard
who he was. Having trouble enough recalling
just the fringes of who I was.

So now, at what by my watch, if they would give it back to
   me,

must be about seven-thirty,
I will not ask anything of any so-and-soing body
in the world . . .
                    Certainly
never to be human . . . The HUMAN RACE!
No, not even for the laughs. The race of
napalm Santa Clauses!
Sheep herded by glib lies that greed concocts,
he-harpies safely out of sight and sound
cheerily showering some thousand tons of bombs
on the innocent helpless to strike back,
pointless despoilers and defilers of what
might elsewise be a fairly pleasant world.

AND YET . . .

Boul' Miche, May 1968

Last night's tear gas still stinging in the air.
Paving blocks still in piles. Girl huddled on the
sidewalk, scalp bleeding, arms covering her face
against the troopers' boots and bludgeons. This
boy not even a spectator   a passer-by on his way
home in the nearby Rue Gay-Lussac. His rush took
the C.R.S. sergeant by surprise   sent him reeling
up against the grill. Wilting beneath the thuds,
the boy   eighteen or so   managed to throw himself across
the girl.
At the *commissariat* revived enough for questioning,

he could only say, "On est français, quoi!"
Not only had never seen the girl before   was not a
student nor even a sympathizer. On the whole against
the lot of them for burning cars and felling all those
trees for barricades   But when cops took to clubbing
girls for fun . . .
They had a police surgeon stitch his head, locked him up
for the night and on his mother's pleading sent him
home.
The concussion and double vision were gone in a month
or so and he went back to the accountant's office where
he worked.
The episode cost the boy his employer's confidence.
He was skipped over for promotion and given to understand
that there was no room for reds in the business.

(Thunderclaps are heard.
Off Scylla a waterspout scours seashells
from the seabed and hurls them above the clouds.
The young English pilot tugs the wheel
and hauls the yoke into his gut.)

Part Two

Don't and Never Did

". . . don't and never did
opt to be human. Given any choice, would rather
have been begotten by a dog-fox on a vixen
or an alley tom on a good mouser . . ."

        Retract? No,
not retract, but put it this way.
You've got to be something—right? Now Zeus—
everyone knows Zeus, the papa of the gods?
He has everything, all the advantages, including being
            purely mythical.
Maketh like a swan and screweth Leda,
maketh like a bull and slips it to Europa—
and keeps his godhead dignity throughout.
Smote the Titans and everybody else
he felt like smiting. Yahweh, Dagon,
Baal, Wodin, Shiva, Moloch,
weren't in the same league with him.
Lick his weight in wildcats without half trying.
Ares the war god, Apollo who flayed Marsyas,
Hermes, were his sons, Aphrodite,
Athena, Artemis among his daughters.

All right, could I be Zeus, I still would choose
rather to be human, to stand beside
certain humans, even from afar. Or if,
impervious as was never any god,

I could be an ultimate grain of sand,
my choice would stay the same.
                      I say this knowing
that soon in some brash, noisome realm
where Pluto-Goldblatts reign, and weary, hurrying,
taut or soggy nurses are all there are
in line of houris, I shall die—
last installment on the price of being man.

           Nobody will administer extreme,
or any other kind of, unction to me,
no Greuze depict my touching deathbed scene.

      Thou ministering vampire, spade-chinned
      oakum-wigged Sairey Gamp of the cobalt age
      (no, I will not believe
      this horny-knuckled, steel-rimmed hagfish hath
      what I shall never touch again or see . . . God
      let it not be so!) aroint thee.
      Let me hold the glass, old spinster spider;
      I know your ways. Uncup your claw
      from under my occiput.
      Aroint! I said. Scuttle back crabwise
      into that foul funnel of your web,
      drawing that musty effluvium of yours behind you.
      Yes, I still want a drink but not that badly.
      Better men than ever I was have died of thirst.

Now, shorn of upper-case and P-for-poor,
"The old bastard in 10-B's been trundled to the morgue.
A nice kid with a slightly fractured whatzis
he got skiing is taking over his bed."

Don't shave and rouge and powder me,
slick down my hair. Don't make me look presentable,
which I never did except young and naked

or all decked out in battle dress with all the ribbons.
Let me look dead and tired and old,
and no one look on me.

Icarus to Eve

Madam, I'm Adam
madA m'I, madaM
Madam, I'm Icarus, your son.
The one who flew too near the sun. Remember? No?

The elder Brueghel sees and sums it all:
not even a ripple in the bright small waves.
Steered by the title, the eye looks twice to find
the limp, unwieldy, disappearing legs.
(The headlong carcass outdistanced breath and sense:
sheer velocity makes instant anesthesia.)
Filling the foreground, the plowman goes about
finishing his chore. The contoured furrows and
horse's humble rump spell order and patience.
A man is fishing from the bank. Beyond,
a gawking shepherd seems to let his flock
tend *him*. A dog of sorts sits at his feet.
Nearby a ship, a fresh wind in her sails,
heads down the estuary. Sailors are on deck
and in the rigging. In this tight cosmos, nothing
notes the splash—except perhaps a rod or so away

one straggling sheep that seems to lift its muzzle
a moment from its grazing. A spring day is ending.
A pale smudged sun is setting in the sea.
Madam, I am Icarus, your son.
Wax melted when I flew too near . . . Remember?
No? There's no wonder. I have so many siblings
that the only wonder is that even
an absent-minded sheep should note our fall.

(Without us, legs would still be fins.
"Johnny! Don't you go too near that land.
You want to get all dry!")

This Stealth

This stealth surrounding dying . . .
       reject from a conveyor bed . . .
           A nod . . . a nod . . .
Checking watch
MR GOLDBLATT makes an annotation

      Leaving more room
until another bed . . .

The Magdalenian man, who graved and painted
those bulls and charging bison on cave walls,
tread on the fossilized remains
of long extinct Solutreans, whose kitchen middens

had piled up on dust or fossil forms
of Aurignacians, one of whom had shaped
the ivory mother goddess of Lespugue.
Before that were Mousterians, who shaped their flints
to fit a solid fist, Acheulians, Chellians,
men of Neanderthal.
    At what point something ceased
being whatever it was and became
        human—
first animal aware
of death—not even the most assiduous
study of a stray molar here and there
will let us say.

Human I never would have chosen to be,
yet grant the poor bastard this: his lust, unlost
for all frustration, to push his way beyond
whatever he is.
    Madam, I'm . . .
        Look, ma! Look quick! I'm . . .

The sheep resumes
    its munching at the grass.

The Christoi*

With hankering for neither laurel nor halo,
his prayer directed to that God
who "need not even exist to reign,"
Baudelaire implored, "Grant me the strength
to do my duty immediately every day
and thus become a hero and a saint."

Hero?   Saint?

Hero is apt to be preëmpted
for such as Achilles, Nelson, Guynemer, Frank Luke.

And *saint?*
Dominic who dearly loved a whiff
of sizzling flesh enhanced by screams?
Olaf the killer from ruthlessness and greed?
Raymond, Thomas à Becket? So many
who neither meant nor did well, at best
wasted their lives in empty rhetoric
and at worst . . .

Hero *and* saint. Prometheus, except for being
slightly more mythical perhaps than some.
A saint who hates the godhead?
(Knowing what would be Zeus's undoing,
he chose rather to have the vulture tear
his liver through the ages than to reveal it
to him and thus prolong gods' tyranny over man.)
The need is for a word to cover all
who try to scale the face of heaven, thieves of fire,
to bring back "secrets for changing life,"

*See glossary, page 202.

every Prometheus, from the Aurignacian
who gouged mammoths in the cave of Arcy
to the man of Amsterdam who painted
the flayed ox carcass, from the one who first
pierced holes in reeds to him who died known mostly
as the sire of twenty children and highly skilled
performer on both organ and clavichord.
(The *great* Bach, most agreed
was Karl Philipp Emanuel.)

A term to fit Saint-Just, age 26 years two days,
standing on the scaffold in his master's blood,
and the boy choosing prison rather than be sent
to murder freedom-lovers half a world away.
Christos (from χρίειν, to anoint)
shall I say. Anointed, elect, chosen.
Chosen by whom?
Why, by themselves, I think.
Settle for christos, christoi.

Yes, *they* did the choosing. Chose once for all
and then again at every moment. Wisdom learned
at every choice making the next choice harder—
and easier!
Cézanne, the banker's son of Aix, along the road
to Le Tholonet, studying la Montagne Sainte-Victoire,
hours on end, day after day,
stopping to wash his brush after every stroke
to keep his mind a fresh blank for that choosing
less choice than discovery.
Proust—one book of a million-and-a-quarter words.
Every image, balancing of shape and sound, intonation,
every pattern of texture or construction,
every rhythm, color, tint, a choice—
a choice yet not a choice. (". . . *we are not free*
before a work of art, we cannot fashion it
to our own wishes. But since it pre-exists us

and is both ineluctable and hidden,
we must discover it
as if it were a law of nature.") Every choice
a choosing (discovering) of self and selves
to *make* the choice. *"Un des moi . . . l'autre moi . . .*
le moi qui venait de renaître . . ." (Unless
ye be born again . . .)
The pampered little pederast chose nameless God
and, choosing God, chose agony and abnegation,
perpetual adoration.
Devoured by the cancer of holy Joy, the blessèd anguish . . .
"cet appel vers une Joie supra-terrestre"
(the *appel* itself is Joy). Consumed,
eaten away by "ineffable Joy . . ."

Péri, facing the firing squad at Mont-Valérien.

Some of them not entirely housebroken.
Pounded on the keyboard with a bootjack
to prove that it was out of tune. (He hadn't heard
a sound these many years.)
Broke his lease because his landlord tipped his hat to him.
His way of eating, particularly in his latter years,
was, shall we say (Grove does), "unbearable."
Spilled ink on the piano.
Shook the rain water from his hat all over
his host's furniture and books.

Maybe he is boasting when he tells of being a successful pimp.
For various reasons—*qui ne m'entent n'a suivy les*
    bordeaulx—
relatively few first-rate poets ever are.
He did, however, kill a priest, take part
in robberies and muggings. Let off from hanging,
"in view of the ill life of said Villon,"
was banished for ten years from Paris and its environs
and never heard of again.

Wiped his muddy boots on the new cretonne curtains.
Stood naked in the window, throwing his clothes
down into the street (because, as he,
country boy of seventeen and never been
in a bourgeois house before, dared not explain
to these belles dames de Paris,
they—the clothes—were crawling with lice
even before he left Charleville).

Some of them are indeed Titans
but I am struck by so many of them
being ordinary men differing from their neighbors
only by speaking out when others are keeping silent,
by saying "No" when others are giving dull assent,
by looking at situations clearly
and acting, within their means, accordingly,
by branding lies as lies.
What did he mean (this insurance executive) by
"The common man is the common hero?"

Caduceus

                    There
        in the meadow   lying on his belly
                                    by the towpath
            grass   new and lush
                        are
        sprinkled   heels crossed above his back
            with pale
                        at least
        flowerets too frail and insignificant
                        19 *ways*
                            to have a name
            he thought
                        of being
        Je EST un
                        shat on
                                autre
                        by
            why not
                as many different
        Je SONT
                        kinds of
                                beaucoup d'autres?
                black birds

    Il n'y avait donc pas de merles en Abyssinie?

Desnos

All bear witness,
some in a warped, obscure, circumvented way,
to human dignity . . .
              (Plenty there are
    one wouldn't care to have around the house
        of a rainy Sunday.)

        "HERE lies buried an unknown chosen one
                marked mostly
              for his various ineptitudes.
        That glow about his head, sometimes mistaken
                for a halo,
        was the buzzing contrail of the Furies."

A scale to judge them by? There is none.
To rate the strength of winds, intensity of earthquakes,
magnitude of stars, yes. To measure, balance, to count
the christoi, no.
"Who? *That* one! Look, I knew him when
he was ghosting papers for ladies' study clubs
and stealing hubcaps to keep himself in gin."

There have been fools and cowards among them—
                touched for the moment—
and those who, having chosen,
went back on their choice.

Desnos, that slope-shouldered juggler-with-sounds
behind his bug-eyed lenses and with his tricky sleight—
I say that, once his life and words caught flame,
he stands among the christoi.

              At Compiègne
before they jammed the prisoners in
200 to a boxcar for a five-day journey
without water or food, the SS ordered
the Communists among them to step forward.
No reason he should do it but he did,
well knowing what it meant.
                            Buchenwald,
the blare and glare, slaps, kicks, curses in ten languages,
roll calls standing at attention half the night in rain,
beatings, starvation, the exhaustion of
shuffling corpses. "Out of all this
I want to make a song . . . an epic poem.
No, a cantata. It has the stuff of a cantata."
Through the month's forced flight—Auschwitz,
Floha, Flossenberg, Terezin,
under the thud of blackjacks and rifle butts,
he clutched the box that held his stub of pencil
and the unfaltering spate of poems.

Delivered by Czech guerrillas from the concentration camp of
Terezin, Robert Desnos died of typhus before he could be re-
patriated. The box in which he carried the poems that he had
written over the last sixteen months of his life was found by a
fellow *Häftling* who, seeing that it contained nothing but scrib-
bled scraps of paper, emptied it and used it to carry his own
scant belongings in. Citations from his poems published in clan-
destinity are engraved on the walls of the impressive Mémorial
de la Déportation, on the upstream end of the Ile de la Cité. The
only poem that his Czech friends salvaged was addressed to
Youki.

It sang in him
Poetry sang in him
Love sang in him
Love and Liberty and love of Liberty

His liberty   your liberty   my liberty
sang in him
and let him die all poet and hero and all saint.
    ("Convertir la haine en espoir.")
His words live on the granite walls
of the staunch, anguished prow that cleaves the Seine:
CAR CES COEURS QUI HAISSAIENT LA GUERRE
BATTAIENT POUR LA LIBERTE AU RYTHME MEME
DES SAISONS ET DES MAREES DU JOUR ET DE LA
                                    NUIT

I wish that those whose deadly smirks mock all
that such men live for
could read it as it stands there, read it
with their eyes and lips and jelly in their bones.
They would not believe it, but there *are*
"hearts that hate war and beat for Liberty."
Crush them in the most savage ways you can devise
and they will still outlive you.
These hearts that "beat for Liberty
to the very rhythm of the seasons and the tides
of day and night" can not be stilled.

Great? Only as thousands like him were.
No stuff there of a solar myth. He was
a boy grown to be a man who did not shrink
from suffering and dying for what he loved.
And, being human, would not allow being made
a walking carrion to diminish his humanity.

Gabriel Péri who died "pour des lendemains
qui chantent." (O doux Jésus! That sing at Ben-Suc?
My-Lai?) No morrow within the span of any now
on earth will ever sing again. All you
who died in *hope* were dupes, though none the less
christoi.

Christos, Van Gogh with his 39 crows
above the wheatfield on the road to the cemetery
of Auvers. Great, absurd Balzac.
Wolfgang Amadeus Mozart, whose letter to
his cousin Anna Maria Thekla read in part:
"Dreck!—dreck! . . . o süsse wort! auch schön
o charmante! . . . dreck, schmeck und leck!"
and more of the same,
which is regrettable but didn't keep him from composing
the Quintet in G Minor—nor Flaubert from saying that
"the three most beautiful things God ever made
are *Don Giovanni, Hamlet* and the sea."
The hand that carved in mammoth-tusk the Venus of Lespugue,
the parturating virgin mother of God . . .
I looked at Alberto Giacometti and saw
the furrowed, Gauloise-smoking monkey face
of one of the christoi.

Christoi all
those whose little donkey-rides
are preludes to Golgothas.

And It Came to Pass

. . . Not so much an anagogic urge
as an impious itch to change
himself, his world, his universe,
without the slightest certainty of bettering them . . .

Choice between
pitying and admiring the poor brute
      we cannot blame
for being caught inexorably in
a process of evolution that has not abated
since first a set of gills
      was turned in on a pair of lungs—
has, on the contrary, acquired more and more momentum.

"Our modern world," Teilhard points out, "has come about
in less than 10,000 years. And in the last
200 years it has changed faster
than in the course of all the preceding millenniums."
He wrote that back in 1941 when there were still
choo-choo cars and atoms were unsplit
and forcing young men to baste babes in napalm
from safe distances would have been considered in bad taste,
the farthest man had ever been from earth was 10.6 miles,
and nobody had set eye on the backside of the moon.

And it came to pass that the Lord God spoke out of the
    mouth
of a Kansas preacher and said unto Luther Burbank,
"If I had meant there to be pitless prunes,
white blackberries, spineless cactus and blue poppies
I would damn well have made them that way."
Now in those days Luther Burbank had confessed
in an unguarded moment that he was not too sure
there really was a God—not that he was an atheist,
just didn't know for sure.
So the Lord God, or so the preacher said,
up and struck him dead to prove He did exist,
the old man being three-score and seventeen.

Burbank was a simple, kindly, unambitious soul
with no yen to get fame or profit out of his "creations,"

as he termed them.
He was not a scientist, had little education,
did not know
an isotope from a neutron
somehow he never even got an honorary degree.
He knew some aspects of nature from having spent
a lifetime puttering around to see what happened.
One would have thought he was the sort of man
God would have liked.
But according to His mouthpiece, No.

"Wizard of Plants!" the obituaries screamed.
"Never in all the history of horticulture . . .
Eight-hundred-odd creations . . . The mind reels
to think . . . One of the greatest
benefactors . . ."

The facts . . . Well, he did develop and name
the Shasta Daisy—"handsome in borders . . .
soon dies out . . . best grown as a biennial."
Most of the other things—pitless prunes, plumcots,
white blackberries—seem not to have caught on,
though, where it has not reverted, jackrabbits
will eat spineless cactus for want of other food.

Good Friday

Hosanna! Hallelujah!
They threw down palm branches all along the way.
(What the owners of the trees and of
the borrowed donkey thought remains unstated.)
Today is Sunday. Four more days to go.
They threw down palm branches. (Who is *they?*
And where were Francis Cardinal Caiaphas
while this was going on, and Pontius X. Pilate?)
    They threw down palm branches, and the donkey
("What was the slipperiest day they ever was?")
gravely setting one neat hoof before another
walked on them.
    I am trying to see the man's face.
    The answer is there, there and in what
he is doing with his hands.
Waving acknowledgment of cheers? Uplifted
in benediction. Raised in a V sign or triumphant
clenched fist? ("The winnuh and still
       champeen . . .")
I cannot see the face.

Descended into hell.
    ("What's slipperest day they ever was?" Tommy, the
      Slovak
spittoon-emptier on the nightshift, used to ask
regularly twice a night. A crafty glint.
"Day Christ go through Jerusalem on his ass. Huh!
Got yuh that time." His only joke in English.
He treasured it until I explained and spoiled it for him.
"Donkey? What's is 'donkey'?" Four legs, long ears,
hee-haw, hee-haw.

In Slovak the word was *vosel*, he said, and looked
    nonplussed.
"Why Christ he's ride a *vosel*—rich guy like him?")

Descended into hell on his ass
and not even his own
Descended into hell through a flurry of ticker tape
Descended into hell   into hell

The Surf

    WHITE NOISE
environs me and bears me up and out
    The Lord is obviously no shepherd of mine
The swirl of
WHITE NOISE . . . surf . . . a grain of sand . . .
    At Finistère in equinoxial storms
breakers will scoop up pebbles and strew
them over the cliff and into parish closes.
Veils of spray sweep miles inland.
Sheep huddle in the fog,
lost together.

This is the fourth day   and no coming forth . . .
    Lazarus, you remember meeting me in hell?
Marsyas, the name is.
"No, I cannot say I do."
    I remember   I remember

I remember only the white
surf roar and the dank spume
of loneliness.
                    Lazarus, do you remember me?
Shadow among shadows, faceless dream
   groping among dreams,
shade circulating among shades
tapping out their ways with white canes.
Midnight. It has always been midnight. Tomorrow is
midnight.
                    Lazarus, don't you remember me?
Marsyas. I am the fellow inmate who whispered to you,
"Today is midnight."
                         And the great horologe
boomed forth the twelfth stroke.
     (Actually it was
     another grain of sand
     trickling in the hourglass.
     This has long been going on,
     the deafening crump
     of a grain of sand trickling in the hourglass.)

My name is . . . My name is . . . hmm . . .
You! You that were resurrected! Do you remember
what I said my name was?   My name is . . .
Adam   Icarus   Marsyas   Ishmael   Merlin

Mélusine, from this dank, jumbled death-bin,
I cry out to you   knowing well
no answer ever will come. (Look goddamn it,
you can write. You know the alphabet, you have hands,
a sheet of paper, pens, pencils, a typewriter.
You have written books. Or don't write. Sign your name.
Or make an X—Mélusine, her sign.)

Black Squirrels and Albert Einstein

Questioned as to the chiefest goal of science,
he sniffed, "To keep the scientist amused."

. . . Communicated little those last years
even with his colleagues. Shunned underwear and haircuts—
and socks, because they only led to holes.
And who needs cuffs? He lopped them off to save on laundry.
No paper handy, he would lie abed
and scribble equations on the sheets.

    "The two-three times you might say we got chatty,
    all he talked about was squirrels—how ours
    in Mercer Street aren't like the ones in the old country.
    Kept repeating. Genius maybe, but he said
    almost the same things every time we talked."

What *is* there you can say to strangers,
to the perennial strangers who live next door
and you see every day?
                "Nice weather"?
                        "Hot enough
for you?"
        "Who do you pick to take the series?"
Or what's wrong with repeating? There are those
who love it. Homer, for all his "strong-greaved Achaians,"
"Hector of the shiny helmet," "Apollo of
the silver bow," still holds his own in paperbacks.
                Or take the case
of Mado, wondrous little whore girl, sweet
presence tinged with shades of Jules Pascin—
and loved her work. (Nothing is—unquote—
work unless you'd rather be doing something else.
Which never happened to her.) Still,

as the song asserts, "they don't make jam all night."
Man is a talking animal. But talk of what?
I tried bicycle races: she had never seen one.
Love: it was too much like talking shop.
Books: she had never read one.
Food: she was no gourmet. Clothes: she spent
her more meaningful moments not wearing any.
I lit on history—Louis Quatorze, at random.
He struck a spark. Louis Quatorze liberating
Brittany. (She came from Plougastel.)
Louis XIV and la petite O'Murphy.
Louis XIV and the retreat from Moscow.
Louis XIV and the rape of the Sabines.
Louis XIV and, oh! that Christmas night
crossing the rivière de la Loire to take
the drunken Hessians—des espèces de boches—
in the rear! Combining, as it did,
Christmas and boating, it was, next to
Louis XIV letting the old woman's cakes burn,
her favorite story. Encore! Encore!
and never change a word. Allons, encore.
    "Et le bon Roi lui dit, 'Bien merci, Mademoiselle
                          Pocahontas.
Tu m'as sauvé de la mort et du scalping.
Je te fais donc Comtesse du Barry . . .'"
    "*Duchesse* du Barry! Tu vois que je ne dormais pas.
I only closed my eyes to listen better.
Encore. The one about the time he shot
the apple off the little Prince's head."

    "All he could talk about was squirrels. No kiddin'—
black squirrels with tufted ears!
Seems in the old country that's how they come."

Yorick

"Nice guys finish last."

Leo Durocher

And those who only floundered, flapped
like oil-sludged gooneys and never did
get wing-borne?

Call him—I knew him well—Yorick, A. P. Yorick.
Slow-spoken, gentle, patient, a good mind,
face of El Greco's *San Luis Rey de Francia.*
"I think that I know how to see. I have
métier, almost as much as any living painter that I know.
Not that that means much. I work hard and every day.
Yet somehow what comes out is not *my* painting—
only a sort of exercise I learned that never quite came true."
Each picture *started* fresh enough. He primed
and stretched his own canvases,
best Belgian linen, Foinet hand-ground paints
(even for sketches, she wouldn't let him skimp).
She sat there in the atelier, knitting, reading,
sometimes herself painting in watercolor, always taking care
not to let her being there disturb him.
She loved to watch him paint—his quiet dedication,
sure touch, taste. That was all she asked
for having had the privilege to give
the funds that left him free to be creative.
Never, although she too had studied at the Slade
before their marriage, did she comment on his work
except to tell him *that* day's work was good . . .
as it often was in the first stages,
before it faltered and went limp and died.

The finished, stifled canvases stacked deep.
Desperate one day, he asked Paul Burlin for advice.

Burlin, who at that time was painting
lopsided incandescent cows erupting
into explosive heavens and convolute siestas
of coveys of lady acrobats,
because he saw and liked them that way,
stood for a moment teetering on his heels
before the latest work, a big one, some
eight feet by six, of three competently done
hieratic nudes. He studied them.
"What are they? Muses? Graces? Fates?"
Just women, Yorick told him. Burlin shrugged.
"Well, maybe they're okay, except they seem to come
from a world where no one ever got a hard-on."
A word that Mrs. Yorick didn't know. When he had left,
she asked what Mr. B. had meant.
And Yorick stammered, "Well, I suppose you'd say
he found them rather parthenogenetic."
She did know what *that* meant and thought it was
the nicest compliment she'd ever heard—
would never have thought that Mr. B., whom up to then
she never quite had liked,
could have such sensitivity.

Read Freud, Jung, Adler. Learning that Otto Rank
lived in Paris, signed up to take a quickie
in ten sessions. One day halfway through,
professed finding his faith begin to wane.
"For instance, what's to keep me from *inventing*
dreams to tell him? Say, something so absurd
no one could dream it—like that I owned
a white elephant that followed me everywhere
I went . . . couldn't get rid of her because
I couldn't bear to hurt her feelings?"
Why not try it on him? I asked. "You mean it?
He wouldn't see that I was spoofing?
Well, I suppose I might."

Next time we met I asked if he had told
the analyst his dream. "What dream? Oh, that.
No. When I tried to I found it was so crazy
I couldn't even remember what it was about."

. . . Ascetic . . . Ate and drank sparingly.
At table sketched to keep his hand in.
. . . and studious . . . austères études . . .
    Uccello's composition
    Degas's rendering of volume as in the
          yawning laundress's belly
    Manet's brushwork,
    the frescos of Tavant
    Gislebertus of Autun
    Hiroshige
always coming back to Rembrandt, Cézanne, Georges de La
  Tour,
Michelangelo, Piero della Francesca. Even learning much
from painters he didn't care much for:
David, Constable, Pascin's erotic line.
Going through Montauban, he stopped off for a week
to study Ingres.

Stillborn canvases stacked against the walls,
ready to be turned face-out and shown
if ever anybody cared to see them.
Seven viae dolorosae to the week
and every night Gethsemane. She would beam,
"From the very first,
my faith in him has never faltered.
His day will come."

Burlin—he was knocking off awards
and selling canvases as fast as he could cover them—
took pity on him.
"Jesus, hombre, I'd quit

painting if I didn't get any more fun out of it than you do.
There's a million ways to make a better living easier."
Yorick's lean El Greco face went instant white.

Yorick a christos? Who's to say?

Masque for Luis Buñuel

Director of *Viridiana* (1961),
The Exterminating Angel (1962),
Belle de Jour (1968), *The Milky
Way* (1969), etc.

1

Pan in priest's livery or archpriest in Pan's.
Cleft hooves are castanets and, rictus in reverse,
even his bluntest jokes will have their subtleties,
impelling voyageurs to slip behind
the heroic statue on the esplanade
of the City's twin titulary goddesses
and, stifling for the instant tears and prayers alike
for the drear living and the luminous dead,
masturbate against the KEEP OFF THE GRASS sign.

2

The realm he reigns in   hopelessly abounds
in answers deftly shorn of questions
Incongruous clarities
unveil themselves at random—

lewd homilies   in flesh and bone,
precisely documented blasphemies.

3

In the strained silence of the blizzard night,
sole stir the blurred   traffic lights
blinking to one another, a mouse
nibbling at the wires set off the
burglar alarm in the delicatessen store
across the street. It rang all night
and well into the dawn
over the untracked, drifting snow.

4

A scream? Pay it no mind.

Tall in her naked ambiguity—
tapered flanks and groove of spine,
the stately callipygian wraith
poses before the pier glass
that gives back no reflection.

5

Hah!
raped by her paternal uncle, rumor says?
Holà! She on the eve of entering holy orders
and he a high hidalgo famed for pious works!

6

A breath stirs the cold ashes on the hearth
of the deserted pavilion.
A Boule horologe, gilt and tortoiseshell,
grinds out the threadbare hour.
It is dawn because a heavy two-wheeled dray
rumbles over dewy cobblestones
to plop of fetlocked hooves.

7
And autumn.
          In Aragon a bandy-leggèd priest,
followed by *vendimiadores*, their baskets slung
across their shoulders,
stumps forth to bless the mountain vineyards.
          ¿Y usted, don Luis, qué tal?

8
               Qué tal, indeed!
O maudlin Minotaur, Proteus, profound,
translucent troglodyte!

9
His devious sobriety provokes silent catcalls,
sniffs, lubricious intentnesses   And look!
down all the aisles, through all the exits,
trampling the usherettes who would restrain them,
people are walking out
               Too late

10
the harm is done.   A gong tolls. Enter the Angel
   of the Lord herding across the banquet hall a flock
   of rams and ewes in heat. Jammed between the
      porphyry posts and banisters of the monumental
         staircase, they flounder upward, the ewes half
            trampled, half mounted, by the rams. Their
               bleats become more frantic, then dwindle. The
                  guests, more famished by the moment, lick
                     their chops and exchange knowing glances.

               "Simon, son of John, lovest thou me?"
               "Aye aye, Lord."
               "Feed my sheep."
               "Yassir. To whom, Lord?"

The Angel appears at the top of the staircase. He brandishes
his flaming sword and triumphantly exhibits a dripping
ram's head. Horns blare.
The spotlight fades to a faint glow. A sudden squall of snow
hides the Angel. When it abates, he is seen wearing the
ram's head and holding his own haloed head aloft in
his hand.
The lights go out. A screen shows a slide of Whistler's
Mother. Gradually she takes on dimension and assumes
the profile of the ram. She sits motionless for several
seconds, yawns widely and loudly.
One after another the guests, now replete, belch, yawn and
fall asleep leaning on each others' shoulders.

11
On a Guinea beach a covey of small cannibals
utters shrill cries and scatters in all directions
before a troop of Franciscan missionaries who,
with loud halloos, their robes tucked up to their knees,
pursue them with gilded bows and arrows, shouting
"Praised be the Lord!" every time
they transfix one to the sand.

12
Good Friday, church bells silent for the day
good Judas will give sway to his good remorse.
The Good Samaritan will lend a length of rope
measured for drop and weight, suggest the tree,
recoup the cost by selling snippets of
hanged-man's lucky noose, more efficacious
than mandrake, four-leafed clover, rabbit's foot.

13
[*Pianissimo*]
To the cadence of martial music
ghosts of the sheep, now resurrected as goats,

parade through the banquet hall, bearing
banners, eagles, croziers. A tuba and a glockenspiel play:
    "Rock-a-bye, baby,
    On a tree top.
    When the bough breaks
    The cradle will drop
    [*How these lines run*
    I do not recall]
    Down will come baby,
    Cradle and all."
[*Fortissimo*]
    DON LUIS!
            [*diminuendo*]
                Don Luis!
                    [*piano*]
                    don Luis . . .
Several seconds pass before a faint echo says:
    Don Luis Buñuel.

    14
He has released a statement to the effect
that this must be the last film he will make,
explaining that he is now too confirmed an alcoholic
to render the murky radiance of
his hallucinatory world.

The Dutch Head Nurse

In the American Hospital of Paris
where three of the doctors and two nurses
        were American,
the happy young Lapland nurse explained,
"Is okay my coontry only is too much cold
and winters is no sun. Is good only for reindeers."

She was no reindeer   rather a bright-eyed
flicker-tailed ibex or chamois
with nimble thighs that only fear of seeming senile
kept me from stroking.
She was tinkering with my transfusion apparatus,
business of trying to make the blood drip faster
but mostly an excuse to babble
in her freshly improvised English,
when another nurse,
squat, middle-aged and fire-breathing,
scuttled in. "What are you doing here!
You have not the right. Only I
may touch these things!" and shooed her from the room.
No sooner gone than the Lapp girl slipped back
"That one is hade noorse. Is Dotch."
She made it rhyme with Scotch, it sounded like a malediction.
"She is not liking me. I am not knowing why.
I am kind and gentle, good.
I am liking all peoples,
but that one, no, she is not liking me.
Truly, I am not knowing why."

And the Veil of the Temple Was Rent

"Nothing I have ever done . . .
   Nothing I have ever done . . .
      Nothing I have ever done . . .
                              was

                    ⎧ paper it was written on
                    ⎪ canvas it was painted on
   worth the   ⎨ clay it was modeled in
                    ⎪ staves it was scored on
                    ⎩ etc.

"Nothing," he said, "thank God, that I have ever done
will last."
          Wrong:
a child cannot drop its rattle from its cradle
without the effect [unquote] being felt
to the outermost fringes of the universe.
True, the infant's name, if that is what you mean,
will not go down in history, nor the effect
necessarily be beneficial—
except as picking up rattles
is good for adults' waistlines.

"Nothing I have ever done
   ELI   ELI
      Nothing I have ever done
         LAMA
            Nothing I ever did
               SABACHTHANI
                  was worth the doing."

By the Watch

10:12 a.m.
I have my watch back. Apparently assured
that I won't swallow it. A busy leisure hour
when mops push lint from under beds.

I am speaking to myself of meaning,
of acts or thoughts merged with or divorced from
each other and words. "Mere symbols." The more mere
they are, the more final, deadly. Symbols . . .
the said thing or even the babbled or unuttered thing
is as committed as the done, or worse.
I am speaking wordlessly of meaning
in its relation to being said.
                              Meaning:
the more you are resigned to letting it
come and remain unintelligible,
though not necessarily for want of words,
the more it twists, contorts itself, to *mean*—
sharply, hardly, cruelly at times
(as if all meaning were not cruel in the end!)

Happening to have a hoe in hand
hilling the asparagus, I killed a snake once,
a new snake, moving out of the stand
of buckwheat into a newfound world, venturing,
gliding in innocent expectation.
I struck and immediately hoped that it was only grazed.
I could not bring myself mercifully—
mercifully—to take another chop
and kill it. Where is the life of a snake anyway?
In the head that cannot close its lidless eyes?
in its length, already severed, that does its best
to stay alive?

("Don't never die till sundown.") Come quickly, sundown.
Come quickly. I will stand beside it,
trying, by covering it with warm dust
as one lays one's coat over a hurt child in shock,
to ease its going.

    "Don't you want your drink now?" No,
I am still working in the garden. (Come quickly sundown.)
    "Aren't you ready to have dinner yet?" No,
I still have things to do.
                 "Can't you sleep?"
No (this unspoken), this day I hurt to death
a young adventuring snake. The spring
is spoiled for me, the summer, the garden
that was to have been beautiful, the year
and years to come.
It was a young handsome thing of grace,
exploring with its flickering tongue the world
it was to live in. If I could be a moment Christ,
my single miracle would heal and resurrect it,
make it forget the anguish that came to it
this day and let it glide once more
out of the buckwheat toward the hollyhocks.

Nothing can forgive me.

Oh, I presumably have killed men, young men perhaps
as handsome as this snake was. I never saw them
through their goggles and windshields close enough to know.
But they were closing in to do their killing too.
Death was a way that they and I had chosen.
Presumably they knew the world they lived in
and what further to expect of it. On the whole,
they got off luckier than I did—
luckier than I did, as they could never know.

Woke each morning expecting to be dead
by nightfall, not too much concerned about it.
    "Man, this here airman's feeling
pretty trepid. No special hunch or anything—
just feeling trepid."

Death with Pants On

"Ace of aces." I saw him once in Harry's Bar
("Tell the taxi Sank Roo Doe Noo")
standing there with an untouched glass before him.
Georges Guynemer, the name had come to stand
beside Jeanne d'Arc's and Roland's. Apart those eyes
and the palm leaves on the ribbon of his Croix de Guerre
reaching to his belt, looked no more godlike
than any other slight tubercular boy of 22.
Not at all the lightning-hurling Zeus
that La Fresnaye's heroic portrait makes him.

Never too sharp a pilot, often shot down,
his Spad riddled, himself eight times wounded.
"But, man, what eyes!" a fellow Cigogne told me.
"And nerve and—well, you've got to say, what luck!"
Two shots—tat-tat—two Fokkers down in flames.
Tat-tat-tat-tat! Tat-tat-tat! Tat-tat-tat-tat!
Eleven bullets: a Rumpler and two more Fokkers.
That night I saw him, his score was 48.
He got five more before his string ran out.

Monday, September 10, sick, irascible,
he had three Spads conk out on him,
force-landed them and met the omen with a tantrum.
Tuesday even his mechanic begged him
to give his crippled luck a chance to heal.
Bright oblivion culled him. His wing-man said,
"One moment he was there. The next the sky
was empty. Not a boche in sight. No flash!"
No trace of either his body or the Spad was found.

Fit apotheosis: the skies of France
his tomb and monument. Streets and schools
named for him, medals struck.

                I think of others
Chapin, Sayre, Comygies, Nick Carter
whom I last saw spinning down in flames
toward La Chaussée. Their first fight—
if you can call it that. Unmatched for unreality:
as we straggled out of clouds into a well
of open sky, the red-nosed hornets swooped.
Most of us
never found a chance to fire a shot.
There were others. I forget their names.

. . . For Approximately the Same Reason
Why a Man Can't
Marry His Widow's Sister . . .

The first time I saw him was at Stella's,
rue Notre-Dame-des-Champs. Apple-cheeked manchild
right out of Satie's *Enfance de Pantagruel.*
Still married to Hadley. (Stella had just left Ford:
this party was to see if she herself
had any friends or if they all were Ford's.)

The last time I saw him was at
Robert Desnos' in the rue de Seine.
He wanted me to meet the ambulances at Le Havre
and smuggle them across the Pyrenees.
(I kept myself available, phoned every day;
nothing ever came of it.)

Youki was there as full and lovely
as a rowdy, randy Ceres. Legally still
married to Foujita, leopardskin-panted painter of
inscrutable nudes that looked like cats
and inscrutable cats that looked like nudes.
"Every time I go to bed with Desnos,
I think, 'Mon Dieu, if we should make a kid,
it would be a little Foujita—long-distance papa
him living in Japan.' Not that him give a damn, but still . . ."
Youki (christened Lucie) who had made history
of a kind in Tokyo by going as Eve
to a diplomatic *ballo in maschera.*

Desnos. Who ever would have thought that out of
word-play, sheer sleight of sound, Pan-piping—
"Mon crâne étoilé de nacre s'étiole—"
sure-footedness as prancing satyrs go,

would come that trumpet voice for blurred
purple dittos:
> "I listen and I hear you, Norse, Danes, Hollanders,
> Belgians, Czechs, Poles, Greeks, Luxemburgers,
> Albanians, Yugoslavs, all our comrades.
> I hear your voices and call out to you
> in a tongue that all men know—
> a tongue whose single word is LIBERTY."

Spoke, called out to Terrorists everywhere,
Terrorists with their home-made bombs that, like as not,
went off at the wrong times and places,
Terroristen who tossed stolen grenades into Soldatenheimen,
who jammed the frogs of railroad switches,
pulled spikes on trestles, found throats with
switchblade knives.
How effectual his message was
is anybody's guess. He died perhaps
the more the saint and hero for having few illusions.

> No handy way to burn a candle to him
> except perhaps to cross the street to Notre-Dame
> and Jeanne d'Arc's shrine. Not quite the same,
> though you can whisper, "A l'intention
> de Desnos et de Youki."

The last time I saw Youki she had been drunk for weeks,
bloated, a stranded whale aground
in Montparnasse where she had reigned
"la plus belle femme de France et de Navarre."
The next time I didn't see her
she was dead.

Berlin. Ernest—not Papa for some years to come—
up from Paris to see the six-day bike race.

Pauline was this time's wife. Dinner with Red Lewis.
A girl—Agatha?—prattled trilingually
of painters. Cézanne? Van Gogh? Picasso?
Juan Gris? Mais c'est à rire! Italians, yes.
But French, Spanish . . . Hemingway stood up and crashed
his fist down on the table. "El Greco is
    a cockeyed GOOD painter!"
The gnädige Fraulein squeaked and subsided mouselike.

    . . . can't marry his widow's sister . . .
12-gauge tranquilizer. At seven o'clock a Sunday morning . . .
having come through the night—and countless other nights.
How long had he been thinking of it? . . . "me a failed
Catholic" . . . thinking even in such terms
as how to pull the triggers?

    No longer apple-cheeked or cheeked at all.
    One WHITE silent bang where head had been.

And how to choose the day when there would be
nothing to be curious about?
    Whether Ordoñez would cut off the coleta,
    whether Anquetil would win the Tour de France again
    and get well hated for it.
    Whether the CIA would succeed
    in setting up a puppet state for Madame Nhu,
    if and when and how any one
    of a thousand events one can't help being curious about
    would happen.

    Curiosity killed a cat. It did? How?
    What cat? Speak no ill of curiosity;
it has kept me living, lo, this many a year.

Minutes out of Naples for Algiers
the soup closed in. Too thick to see the wing-tips,

too high to buck above it. "Any chance,"
I asked, "of turning back?"
                      "None that I'd care to take, sir—
what with Vesuvius and all."
He flew the deck so tight spume caked the windshield.
Then a sudden clearing, there it was—
dead ahead a waterspout, mean and hungry,
a sky-high, belly-dancing funnel. Velocity enough
to drive a copper rivet through armor plate.
Can you split-ass a war-weary C-46?
The British are good people to be scared with.
This young Limey set her on one wing
and yanked the yoke into his belly.
                            (The answer is:
Yes, if you have to, but better not
have to more than once a lifetime.)

"God, this isn't praying. This is just to say
I'd hate to die before I learn
what happens to Mussolini."

    (*What happened came some six months later.*
    They strung his carcass up by the heels.
    Not pretty but quite real. Nothing phony this time
    Absolutely last appearance . . .
    A pity though he couldn't have stuck around
    "to get the beauty of it hot.")

Not Dawn Yet

Not dawn yet   or ever
though the silence is no longer white and blank
    and has somewhat abated
          (The square-bottomed nurse says,
             "Look, if those bars really bother you . . .
             We aren't supposed to
             but if I was just so busy I forgot . . .")
somewhat abated
    Nor is the protracted CUBE as absolute
        nor the click so irrevocable.

Think back,
    Now that the grass is rippled by the rain
and the disk of sun blurred by harbor haze
    Now that Daedalus has put aside his mourning
and the sheep gone back to mumbling its cud,
think back.

      ". . . rather have been sired by a dog-fox
      on a vixen or an alley tom on a good mouser . . ."

Would never have opted to be human?
A bootless speculation. Truths have a way
of not existing short of paradox.

To say that life is good would be to wring
all meaning from both words.
Renan with his "charmante promenade
qu'il m'a été donné d'accomplir à travers la réalité."
Yes, to Desnos too was given
a charming stroll to take—though through a
                 slightly different reality.

From Buchenwald to Floha to Terezin
is not too many kilometers as the crow flies,
but that was not their mode of travel.
The villagers protested at having all those corpses
strewn in the ditches along the way.

Death already on him when freedom came.
Temperature never less than 39.6 degrees.
Alena Tesarova, his Czech nurse,
brought him a wild rose blossom. The petals fell
at his first touch. He would not part with it,
kept it with him into his final coma.
Having this prickly twig a kindly fighting-girl
had given him was good. Having lived through
to liberty was good. Being a poet,
being a man was good.
Did that mean life was good? Had been? Is?
Allons, mon p'tit! Non, mais tu veux rire!
But being human, yes, at times . . . at times
when men are human.

No, I would not secede.
Not for all the Himmlers, Johnsons, Quislings,
Calvins, Torquemadas. I would not secede
even if I could be a grain of sand,
sovereign and absolute
(". . . a grain of sand is almost indestructible. It is the ultimate
product . . . the minute hard core of mineral that remains after
years of grinding and polishing . . . Even the blows of heavy surf
cannot cause one sand grain to rub against another.")

       Choose rather
to be however distant
kin of the christoi, of their race,
sharing their vulnerabilities and servitudes,

privileged to owe reverence to such as
Beethoven, Sisley, Wm. Blake, Chardin, Giotto,
Dr. W. C. Williams of Rutherford, N.J.,
Villon, "povre mercerot de Renes," Arrigo
Beyle, Milanese, Domenico Theotocopuli,
Ravel—"Yes, a success no doubt"
(speaking of the *Bolero*) "though unfortunately
totally devoid of music." All of them . . .
Yes, the Yoricks, the gaunt, undaunted Yoricks.
All the race of blundering doers and undoers
of their destinies, the fumblers, the tanglers of their skeins,
the Masters, whose common anguishes we,
dazzled by their glories (invisible to them),
cannot see.

Arnaut Daniel (circa 1190)

> *Ieu sui Arnautz qu'amas l'aura*
> *E chatz la lebre ab lo bou*
> *E nadi contra suberna*
> Arnaut Daniel

My name is Marsyas. Everyone has heard
of how I challenged Apollo, my flute
against his harp. Midas, whom we had agreed on
as judge, gave *me* the prize. The Romans
put my statue in their forum, symbolizing
Liberty. My name is Marsyas. I bore away the prize
over Apollo, god of music.

Arnautz am I.
I reap the wind, ride an ox
to course the hare and swim against the torrent.

I am Marsyas. There is another version.
This time the Muses—his stable—were the judges.
When they gave *him* the prize,
he trussed me to a tree, flayed me alive.
Choose your own version. I am a crude,
goat-footed, flute-playing, wineskin-sucking
lout that would as soon
screw a Muse as look at her. Sooner maybe.
Depending how she looked.

I, Arnaut Daniel, was born at Ribérac.
I am one honest-to-God *good* poet.
Parchment is dear. Most monks are lunks.
Nobody else can read. What is there to do about it?
Niente. Absolutely *nada.* A couple of years from now
it will be spring again
and I shan't be around to see it.
Willows budding in the meadow, gentians,
jonquils in the woods, girls twittering
in patches of sunlight by the river,
giggling and squealing and hiking up their petticoats
thigh-high to wade ankle-deep trickles in the field,
and I not be there. I've had this cough since Sicily,
gone to make songs for Richard Lion-Heart.
Ten years from now nobody will have heard of me.
    Not only as a poet. *Shove poetry!*
One way or another, it has kept me eating
most of my life. But shove it all the same.
What I'll miss is girls stooping by the brook,
picking cowslips, raising their arms
to put them in their hair and show the sweet
profiles shaping out with spring.

Aï! given a few springs more and even the spawn
of my own loins won't ever have heard my name.
Their mammies will have told them,
"Your pappy was a travelin' man," or
"You are the offspring of a foreign dignitary
who, hearing of my beauty, sent his emissaries . . ."

Ieu sui Arnautz qu'amas l'aura.
Today a brown dog lay sleeping in the sun
outside the tavern. I said, "Hello, dog."
Without bothering to open his eyes,
he beat the warm dust with his tail.
I am Arnaut. I shall be planted in the ground before
that chestnut sapling first bears fruit.

    If you want to see
something of what my eyes have seen,
go down to Moissac's abbey—the twenty-four
Elders with their white robes and golden crowns
and burnished lutes and rebecs, the Christ in majesty,
the cloister. Moissac or Dalon or Cadouin
if they are still standing. Conques, Montsalvy.
Go down to Beaulieu in Dordogne;
the tympanum there shows the Last Judgment
with Jews lifting up their robes
to show the sign of their covenant with Jehovah.
I am Arnaut Daniel. I lived
in a not too unlovely world.

      Mr. Bodington, President of the
      British Chamber of Commerce of Paris and
      authority on Romanesque architecture of
      central, south and western France, said,
      "Browning was not a gentleman. I am surprised
      you should have read him."
      Questioned, he explained, "Why, the fellow was—

uh, no need to cite specific
instances—uh, vulgar, so to speak."
   (Something I must have missed.)

Anabasis

1

And the more he rode, the farther he went;
that was a peculiarity of his.
People spoke of him respectfully
and wondered why.
Sycophants laid his wife while he was out
transplanting geraniums. And wondered why.
Foundations awarded him grants and wondered why.
For a while, he too wondered why and then
gave up wondering and decided
either that it was very natural,
seeing that that seemed to be the way things were,
or that he and they and everybody else that counted
were crazy—which seemed to be perfectly natural too,
although he wondered why.

The conductor came lurching down the aisle and said,
"Say, don't I seem to remember seeing you somewhere,
ol' sport?" and wondered why.
He himself wondered where he was going and why.
With age, wisdom grew upon him:
he merely wondered why he wondered why.

2
This
Puerto Rican kid sat on the front stoop
and ran his fingers across the strings
of the guitar his older brother was in jail for stealing.
After a while he sort of got the hang of it
and it sounded pretty good to him.
There were people going by in the street.
He wondered if any of them would hear it and remember.
Pretty good considering that he didn't know how
to tune it, had never tried to play
any instrument before and had no ear for music anyway—
which didn't make for too much to remember.

Ismael? Soy Marsyas, tu hermano de sangre.
¿Te acuerdas de mí?

(¿Melusina, te acuerdas de mí?)

Apocalypse

All precautions have been taken:
lampposts have been strung with garlands,
wreaths hung about the necks of statues,
certain graffiti that have of late appeared
on the walls of public buildings been effaced
and plainclothesmen posted to apprehend
their skulking perpetrators.

As a temporary measure for her own security,
Cassandra, put under adequate sedation,
has been allowed to repose her vision
in a comfortable subterranean retreat with padded walls.
The city fathers wear happy smiles even when shaving.
The priests cannot recall a time when the auguries
have been so favorable. Poverty, anxiety, fear
are soon to become obsolescent words.
Plans have been drawn up for a municipal festival,
field day, barbecue and Old Timers' Day in one,
with men's and women's barrel-rolling contests on the pond
and potato- and three-legged races with special prizes
for senior citizens of both sexes and toddlers under four.
Miss Meeker's Antiquity Shop is going to provide
an old-fashion hurdy-gurdy and Reverend Stythe
is going to disguise himself in a monkey suit and pass the cup.
The weather man has promised to coöperate.

Yet even in this atmosphere of merriment and thanksgiving,
we should be less than candid did we not confess
to having played doubly safe, taken precautions
against all possible eventualities.
We have—need we say more—propitiated
certain divinities, interceded with certain
ominous omens not to be sooth.

SCENE: *The Fair Grounds. The Mayor is standing on a plat-
form draped with bunting.*
"Friends, Neighbors, Fellow Citizens of this fair—
or should I say, *fun*-fair—city, I want to say
that this is the happiest and proudest day that we have known
since the ostracism of Aristides . . ." (*Approving boos.*)
Sounds of hurdy-gurdy, steam calliope, and
High School Marching Band. Cheers and wolf-calls as
Gerty Brukstis, who has already won the sack-race,
wins the junior strip tease by a split decision,

Reverend Stythe casting the deciding vote.
The only note of discord comes when it is discovered
that, to comply with safety regulations, the rifles
used in the clay-pipe shooting contest are firing blanks.
The antique motorcar event is won by
a souped-up, steam-driven Cugnot 1769
over a 1906 Stevens-Duryea.

GERTY BRUKSTIS, *as Little Red Riding Hood:*
"All right, buster. Just one though, and don't give me
                    mononucleosis."
THE WOLF, *whispering in her ear:*
"That's not all I'd like to give you, baby."

Titters, giggles, sniggers, squeaks and squeals.
        [*A siren*]
        WE INTERRUPT THIS PROGRAM TO ANNOUNCE
        THAT, AS OF RIGHT NOW, THINGS DON'T LOOK SO GOOD . . .
        FLASH JUST IN FROM RHODES:
            COLOSSUS ON THE LOOSE!

Citizens turn to each other uncomprehendingly.
"What's it all mean? What's it all about?"
"You been following it?" "Roads? What roads?
I been saying all along that traffic . . ."

The High School Marching Band strikes up
"There'll Be a Hot Time in the Old Town Tonight."
MAYOR: "Stythe! Make 'em stop that goddam music!
Get everybody out of here!"

Mayor and Councilmen hurry offstage.

COLOSSUS WALKS   [COL
    COLOSSUS WALKS   [OS
        COLOSSUS WALKS   [SUS]

A bulk of silent thunder prowls the streets.
Walls reel on their foundations, towers sway.
It sweeps so low it scallops curbs
      and parapets of bridges.

Colossus walks. His brass feet clang on pavements.
His lungs roar, his breath flakes slates from roofs.
His brazen tufts of eyebrows twang.
His bronze enameled eyes see nothing before them.
His massive pubic mane is an untuned
deafening Æolian harp plucked by a whirlwind.
The brazen balls that ships were wont to pass beneath
clang doom at every stride.
The fluted folds
of an aurora borealis rustle in the black sky
behind his head and shoulders.

Let no man dare behold his face
nor any woman glance long at his loins.
Let no one frame a query in his mind.
Let no man hope: hope, overt or secret, is forbidden.
Let us smother babies in their cradles lest
their whimperings or coos distract him.
Do not cast flowers in his way: he does not care for flowers.
Nor palm leaves: he does not care for palms.
Only let our youths and girls—those carefully chosen,
those only without blemish—cast themselves
silently before Him, their prostrate bodies
carpet His way.

    (Orders have gone out to throttle
    Cassandra in her cell this night.)

BUT WAIT! HEAR THIS!
A miracle! although the Temple
and all the other idols were destroyed,

one statue, that of the Supreme
Vestal, though toppled from her shrine,
is scarcely chipped!

Let us decree a day of solemn prayer
to thank that Power who has vouchsafed this sign
to us in this our desperate hour of need.

COLOSSUS STRIDES. HIS INCANDESCENT SHADOW
TURNS CITIES INTO SMOKING RUBBLE.
FORESTS ARE ASHES. ONLY BONES
MARK THE COURSES OF DRIED RIVER BEDS.
THIS STATION IS SIGNING OFF FOR LACK OF ANY SURVIVORS.

 From deep in the ruins of the city
 a jukebox is playing:
  ". . . Praise Him all creatures here below.
  Praise him above, ye heavenly host . . ."
 The needle is apparently stuck in the groove.
  "Praise Him above . . . above . . . above . . . "

A seething wind leaves lava bubbles in its wake.

The Brocken

 Guess it to be night again because the stocky
 Shetland-pony nurse is back and MR GOLDBLATT gone.
 She takes blood-pressure. "Java goo' day?"

Lady, I had one—thank you—gawdawful day.
She has plugged her stethoscope into her ears
and heareth not.

"in the island that is called Patmos"

SCENE: A blasted—but *really* blasted—heath in the Harz
Mountains. Heaps of remains of what a short time back was
sophisticated weaponry lie about. Front center, an Army
Chaplain. He is obviously in a state of shock, delirious and
very drunk. His body is covered with more third-degree burns
than uniform. Other than this, he is doing very well. When
he had a face, it was probably a pleasant one. The blast
having vaporized all iron rations, he has been living for some
days on a diet of communion wine and wafers. He staggers,
waving a chalice. The thirst of his evaporation is agony. He
raises the chalice, gulps and sings:

> *"The mountaineers have hairy ears.*
> *They're hardy sons-of-bitches.*
> *They wipe their ass with broken glass*
> *And care not how it itches."*

He takes another gulp and addresses the non-audience:
"Oh, hi there, folks. I know you're out there somewhere
even if I can't see you. Might's well get to know each other.
Shouldn' wonder 'f we're the las' folks here on earth."
He gropes for his dog-tag and reads it by touch.
'Capt. Mephistopheles, U.S. Chaplain Corps.' That's right.
Joplin, Missouri. Spirit of denial.
Only I ain't denying nothin' anymore."

He drains the chalice and starts to sing again:
    "The mountaineers . . .
I'll say we're hardy, us mountaineers! Real hardy!
Bein' up here on this mountain . . . that and bein'

born and raised in the Ozarks . . . makes *me*
a mountaineer, I guess. Hardy! Live on maybe
for days yet. Lungs in cinders, burnt flesh
sloughin' off my bones. Can't breathe but still
can sing I guess you'd call it.
Hardy. Maybe live on for hours yet . . . or minutes."

He totters, sways, spreads wide his arms
to try to keep his balance.

A gigantic shadow, luminous and accompanied by
a rainbow nimbus,
cast on the cloud bank by the setting sun,
reflects his movements.*
Even after he drops dead,
the glow seems to linger on a moment
before slowly fading out.

The Red Virgin

> *Ceux qui savent tes vers mystérieux et doux,*
> *Tes jours, tes nuits, tes soins, tes pleurs, donnés*
> > *à tous,*
> *Ton oubli de toi-même à secourir les autres,*
> *Ta parole semble aux flammes des apôtres . . .*
> > Victor Hugo à Louise Michel, 1871

---

* This phenomenon is known as a Brockengespenst (Specter of the Brocken) for having been first observed on the Brocken in the Harz Mountains in 1780.

The portrait in the encyclopedia is kinder
than most. The black dress she always wore did not
exactly set her off. No, for all Verlaine's
ballade: "Louise Michel est très bien,"
she looks amazingly like our own Abe Lincoln—
The nose and forehead, the generous strong mouth.
Only her eyes, wide-set and deep, are beautiful.
What do you know of her except that a Métro station
bears her name and that she was called la vierge rouge?
Simple annal: born to a servant girl
by the master of the château (though some say by his son)
raised in the family, given a good education
she supplemented later with higher mathematics,
physics, chemistry, geology and such,
she qualified to be a teacher but refused
to take the loyalty oath. Heading a private
school, between her teaching and her charities,
she made time for politics and poems—among her best
an ode to our John Brown.
                              When Paris was surrendered
to the Prussians and besieged by Thiers—
Frenchmen fighting Frenchmen, she joined the defenders,
led attacks. (Under an artillery barrage,
she scaled a crumbling wall to save a cat.)
At the end—"we were seven at the barricade,
then three"—a rifle butt knocked her unconscious.
While her captors were busy looting houses,
she came to and walked away. Gave herself up
when the victors proposed to shoot her mother in her stead.

At the court-martial the charge was wearing a uniform,
bearing arms and using same, approving
the execution of two generals.
The prosecutor called for a death sentence.
Her clear voice rang out: "I will not
defend myself. I refuse to be defended.

Since it is clear that the one right allowed
to hearts that beat for liberty
is a slug of lead, I demand my share."

Presiding Judge: "I refuse to hear you further."

Louise: "That is all I have to say.
If you aren't cowards, you will kill me."

Deported to New Caledonia, half a world away,
four months on shipboard in a cage, she writes
not of the hardships but, like a child
on a first journey, of all the wonders:
the sea itself, fresh winds, the mighty storms—
later of the birds and animals, insects,
huge handsome spiders and curious plants.
She learns the Canaque language, teaches natives.

Back in France after nine years of exile,
once more takes up her battle for a world
with neither slaves nor masters.
Packed off to prison on the old complaint
the High Priest Caiaphas made to Pilate,
"He stirreth up the people," she accepted pardon
only "because in prison I am useless;
if they think their grace will muzzle me,
they're wrong." Wherever there were listeners
she spoke. She packed theatres. A bigot's bullet
in her skull was not enough to make her miss
her next engagement.
                    In her spare time she wrote:
quantities of poetry, tracts, science fiction—
including a draft of 20,000 *Leagues under the Sea,*
which one day, needing money, she sold to Jules Verne
for a hundred francs—novels, plays—one
produced in London, memoirs, a history.

Oxford, Algiers, Amsterdam, Geneva, Glasgow.
Nearing 75, she was stoned in Brittany,
carried on the shoulders of workers in Poitou.

She died possessed of a few trinkets and piles
of manuscript. The procession following
her plain pine coffin took nine hours to pass.

People Walking

To M.L.R.

Here is a riddle: Here are people walking,
not to get to anywhere except, if their feet hold out,
back to where they started from.
Walking not for exercise or pleasure,
thousands of people most of whom have never seen
each other before today. Nobody is paying
or obliging them to walk. It makes no sense.

The rain is slackening to a drizzle.
Hour after hour, these men and women filing by
in quiet ranks. Some of them carrying
placards, banners, banderoles.
They spell each other off at holding up the staffs.
Many of them have walked in from distant suburbs
to walk here in the rain this afternoon
and then walk home again tonight.
Men and women. How many of them are there?
(*L'Humanité* will call them half a million:

Le Figaro estimates them at twenty thousand.)
Walking by twenty-odd abreast for hour on hour.

Many of them remember barricades
of café chairs and tables, overturned pushcarts,
cars, autobuses, garbage trucks. They brought out
their own bedsteads and sofas, hoping they would not
get too much smashed, and tossed their mattresses
down from windows. Mostly, their only arms
were what they got from Nazis they could kill.
To many of them, Auschwitz, Belsen, Neuengamme
are more than names. To some of them
Madrid, Teruel, Guadalajara, the retreat
across the Pyrenees, where they learned
all causes are lost causes, are fresh memories.

They are walking, not marching,
a Communist cell-leader beside a priest,
a world-known architect and critic keeping pace,
for all his eighty years, with lean Algerian laborers
and Vietnamese students. A two-star general
walks beside a woman in a blue work-smock.
In side streets along the way, detachments
of police with weighted capes and billies and gendarmes
with carbines stand by in case of trouble.
                                             No need.
When the walkers reach this point along the way,
section leaders turn and raise their arms;
all talk stops. I wonder why. A woman on the curb
calls out, "Bravo, mon général!" He puts a finger
to his lips, nods toward a sign I hadn't seen:
HÔPITAL: SILENCE. "Ah, pardon!"
she whispers. "Pardon, mon général."

The unmeasured tread of all these feet
has found itself a rhythm. My pulse beats to it.

I fall into the ranks. My voice joins
in the anthem the Red Virgin sang in prison.
A tall and very black Senegalese
hands me his pole to carry while he stops
to fix a broken shoelace. For the moment
I am an auxiliary of

```
*   *   *   *   *   *   *   *   *   *   *   *   *   *   *   *   *   *
*   LES TRAVAILLEURS NOIRS DE BOULOGNE-BILLANCOURT   *
*   *   *   *   *   *   *   *   *   *   *   *   *   *   *   *   *   *
```

When we arrive at the Place de la Bastille,
somebody makes a speech that no one hears.
Once more we sing the anthem:
     "C'est la lutte finale.
       Groupons-nous et demain
       L'Internationale
       Sera le genre humain."

These are good people.
They want Vietnam to be free
and Algeria and Greece to be free
and France and America and every other country in the world
to be free. It is as simple as that.
They don't believe that walking in the rain
will *make* them free. But what else can they do?
This will say they *want* them to be free.

These are good people. They do not believe
what they are told to believe. They remember for themselves
what they have learned and known.
Living is not wasted on them.
They are good and brave people.
They have faith without hope
or hope without faith, or both without either.
They see no virtue in being gullible.

These are good people,
these people that I have walked with a little while.
These are brave people. As long as I am with them,
I too am brave and good.
These are innocent people. (There is no wisdom
short of innocence.)
While I am walking with them,
I too am innocent.

We are dispersing now.
The rain is setting in again.

I step into a doorway for shelter.
A woman says, "My dogs are killing me.
If I took my shoes off now, I'd never get into them again.
I can see myself walking from here to Saint-Denis
in stocking feet.
Mais on était beaucoup, hein! Dites donc!
How many would you say? Fifty—a hundred thousand?
Lots of us. It was really worth it."

Her job is punching tickets in the Métro;
her husband is a baker. That's why
he couldn't come today. He needs his sleep.
They have three kids that they are going to see
get decent educations.

"Visse, Scrisse, Amò."

Arrigo Beyle, Milanese

Me too. At random for the lives I lived.
Whose? Mostly good ones in any case.
At moments I have heard the opaque silence
that Giotto knew, the rock's reply to rock,
confirmed, made holy, by the sky. I have guessed
how wood and copper, china, felt to Chardin's touch,
have walked in quiet ranks with men and women
willing to die for what they knew
their dying could not save. At times I have seen
the freshness of the flood that morning
at Port-Marly through Sisley's eyes. I have waked
beside Valérie Marneffe, unlaced the stays
of Odette de Crécy. Pockets clanking with
"all sorts of arms and pistols," I have been
seduced up the ladder to her bed
by Mathilde de la Mole.
I have seen, death in my soul, the desperate beckoning
trees near Hudimesnil. I have breathed
Provençal noon through Vincent's nostrils.
                              Vicariously?
No more than when a Sopwith disintegrated
at a thousand feet with me in part of it—shreds of memory:
avoiding names, pretending that I knew
everybody who seemed to know me. At mail calls,
none ever for me took figuring out.
"Who was your letter from?" "My folks."
(Everybody, even that ape Raz, it seemed,
had "folks." I asked him. A mother, sister, aunts,
he said. "Why? Did you think I was generated in a test tube?"
                    No more vicarious
than whatever put those ribbons on my battle jacket.
No more than me, drop-out from night-school,
delivering the Honors Address at the Phi Beta Kappa banquet,

title, "Whosoever increaseth knowledge
increaseth sorrow," which the toastmaster cut down
to "The Purposes of Learning." Sometimes
running across a mention of
"this distinguished educator," I say,
"It seems to mean you, P.O.B."
It leaves him unimpressed. His greatest source
of lasting satisfaction: having contrived
to get a Paris street named for Saint-Just.

        Gamut of goddesses, tear-channeled cheeks
        and rough-hewn, yearning vulva of Rosmertha,
        mother, sister, mistress of the dead.
        Ishtar, Epona, I have drunk your milk and tears.

. . . cone of light in my eyes . . .
        All this is happening.
Lazarus, remember? I asked you for my name . . .
Thanks for refusing me an answer.

        Finis terrae . . .
Pen-Marc'h, horse's head.

. . . wandering among the stands of menhirs.
Some of them have eyes and concave cones
        to mark the breasts
cups and crosses
The drizzle has set in again   The dead move freely here.
I might speak to them   Gulls
and cormorants already answer.

        We have lived strangers' lives
        in depths and breadths of worlds they lived
        and died to make.

Lull in the gale.

Voices break as waves against a vaster
                finis terrae.
Boom of rumbling rocks hurled against the headland,
rattle of receding pebbles and water swirling—
race and undertow
gathering never-spent strength
to pound again   Spray falling in heavy curtains.
Boom of earth trembling with the shock
      felt a day's walk inland.
Sheep huddle in the fog.

                The dead are very near
            They move freely
                    We talk together with no
            need of words

           The storm speaks.
It sings in me
      the litany of the christoi,
the named and unnamed, the forgotten, though not less
           close for that,
the unknown, the dead who are living
           their fullest lives now:
the man who set his feel of deer
      swimming a freshet
on the walls of Lascaux, he who somehow—
swimming, crawling, working his way vertically up
through darkness—came to paint the bison
in the caves of Niaux,
Louise Michel with her great spate of love—
and hate where hate was needed. Stendhal, "hussard
de la liberté." They who made
Falstaff and Charlus, Hulot, Pickwick.

Marsyas, do you remember me? Ishmael.

Strangers? Selves! Blood brothers.

"And the Evening and the Morning . . ."

(For some time a humming sound has been going on. It
is augmented by the Voices mumbling to each other. By
now it is so loud that Marsyas, who is standing in the middle
of the stage in a hospital bathrobe, has given up trying to
speak.)

A SHATTERING WHITE SILENCE BLINDS AND
      BLOCKS OUT EVERYTHING.

     (Now the Voices and the masks they issued from
     are gone. The young night nurse from the Intensive
     Care Ward is sitting cross-leggèd on the floor to the
     right of Marsyas. He doesn't notice her presence.
     She is listening, though too tired, as she always
     is at dawn, to try to understand what he is saying.
     Marsyas is talking to the self that he has more or
     less found.)

"I am called Marsyas and Merlin
I am called Ishmael and Icarus
My hide hangs on a thorn bush in Thessaly
The spells I taught her still imprison me
in a copse of the forest of Broceliande
Those are my limp lifeless legs that the sheep sees
     splashing into the harbor
Evenings at the water hole I lap with jackals
We snarl but make room for each other
We share our kill   Hagar before she died
taught me to make slings and harden
sharp sticks in fire
     [Shyly] I am also called Yorick."

Strange, the first several times I saw

Rembrandt's *Flayed Ox*, I somehow missed the girl
peeping in the doorway. I still can't guess
why she is there, though I am glad she is.
At Rampillon, if you look close enough,
on the gablet of a wall buttress you can make out
a fool in motley raising a stick to beat
a leashed ape. On the tympanum of a chapel in the fields
near Espalion, Hell and Heaven are switched around
from left to right, and the God presiding this reversed
Judgment Day is definitely horned, as horned
as any Minotaur. Frieze of the apse in that mountain village
where an old woman coming out of mass
and seeing me, a stranger, grabbed my arm and urged,
"Don't look at that, monsieur! Oh, no!
You mustn't look at that!" pointing, stabbing
her finger toward a basalt woman
grinning up from between sturdy legs
at her pronounced pudenda.
                         The queens of Chartres.
Blood-dripping fangs of Durga. Blessèd incongruities,
blends of majesty and bawdry, tenderness and horror—
and innocence.

    (There in Mercer Street his thought ran thus: ". . . the
    mysterious . . . the fundamental emotion that stands at the
    cradle of true art and true science . . . The experience of
    mystery . . . this knowledge and this emotion that consti-
    tute true religiosity.")

The chiefest goal of science?
If he had said, "To grope toward God,"
they would have *known* that,
like all lovers of liberty, beauty, justice—
the man was crazy.

Judgment Day

> "And—what is more significant—he [the votary]
> calls himself by the very name of his god—he is
> himself Bacchus."
>
> Encyclopaedia Britannica,
> 14th edition, "Mystery"

The VOICES, *speaking through three huge terra-cotta masks
   that fill most of the backdrop:*
You who have passed through there lately,
what was it like?
Glutted vultures on dead branches of blighted trees?
Labyrinthine gulch of milling blind and mad
and all the seeing-eye dogs frothing with rabies
and slashing at each other's throats?
Corpses devouring the living piecemeal?
No one able to reach and touch another
except to carry pestilence or doom?

MARSYAS, *who is somewhat identified with Silenus, Bacchus:*
Something of that. That perhaps is one way
it may be seen.

The VOICES:
One way? Perhaps? This from *you*
who saw your bloody hide draped on a thorn bush?

MARSYAS (*He speaks casually, not trying to give a cogent
   answer. He seems to be in a waking trance and communi-
   cating only with, groping for, himself.*)
Did dawn come? I suppose it must have.
Did they give me back my flute and skin?
   No two grains of sand?
The day I came to stand by Eucharis's tomb,
Freya laid her arms about my neck
And kissed me through our tears.

My name is Marsyas. I played a flute.
Forget that silly challenge. I played it best alone,
sitting on a rock or sprawled on banks of wolf's-foot,
checkerberries.
A chipmunk now and then would sit up and listen,
a rabbit froze, ears flat along its back,
after a while went on with nibbling.
A bluejay cocked its head and gave a squawk.
Once a box-turtle opened up and stretched
its wattled neck in my direction.
Nothing of an Orpheus about me. Not charmed,
only at length reassured that this beast with
its different kind of noise
was as harmless as a nickering horse.

The VOICES:
Enough maundering. Look, you left your hide there.
Tell us about the Harpies, the Erinyes,
Medea murdering her children. What about . . .

MARSYAS, *breaking in and speaking directly to the* VOICES:
Cruelties, stupidities, vileness a-plenty.
Filth, indignities, cowardice. What man
can say he never had a share in them?
Haloed lies gloated as they sniffed
burnt offering that we made them.
Brutalities claiming greed for their excuse.
Ishmael did well to take into his heart the cry:
"Woe to him who, in this world, courts not dishonor!"

(*A roar of bloodthirsty hymns accompanied by organ peals and
trumpets is heard in the distance.*)

"The Son of God goes forth to war
A kingly crown to gain.
His blood-red banners stream afar.
Who follows in his train?"

"Onward, Christian soldiers, marching as to war."

"Christian, up and smite them,
Counting gain but loss.
Smite them, Christ is with thee,
Soldier of the Cross."

                    Yet
there is innocence to be found there,
vast innocence of Einstein, Rembrandt, Blake,
Louise Michel, innocence that may be contagious,
innocence of the friend I have called Yorick.
Innocence of those who dare to take
strangers into their hearts and make known their love
with small tokens made, like as not, with their own hands.
Innocence of those who truly speak their minds—
        appalling innocence
of those who make no show of honoring idols
and recognize their God by the completeness
                    of His suffering.
Radiant innocence of the young man sitting beside
his young wife and talking of their chance
of going to prison for making known
their unwillingness to share in crime.

There is the innocence of the man no longer young
who dares speak sense to the mob of sly, malicious idiots
with stones and bottles clutched behind their backs,
who dares pit truths against their jibberish.

   ("And when the battle's over, we shall wear a crown!
   We shall wear a crown! we shall wear a crown!
   And when the battle's over . . .")

we shall be damn lucky if we still
are wearing heads.

Our God is innocent. He holds forth such awards
as only the very innocent could ever prize.

The Making of the Bear

Perhaps for fear of saying to oneself,
"Why you rather than another?" or asking
why it should be done at all,
it is not good to plan such things too long.

No question others had more craft than I.
I had waited for the Old One to give the sign
to one of us, half hoping still his choice
might fall on me. But lately he had turned
to graving stags and reindeer on bits of antler,
art that for all his pains my clumsy fingers
could never seem to master. In any case,
his choice for cavern walls ran to pregnant cows,
bison and ponies. That, and more and more
he favored places not too hard to get at.
"What's the harm in having good work seen?"

Meanwhile the first full moon of spring was near.

    I can't say why I chose the cave I did.
Passing that way one day, I'd seen it
and taken it for a badger's hole until
I saw an owl rise from it and, listening close,

caught the voices of the water.
I set out before dawn and took along
well-scorched moss and tallow, stone lamp, firestick
in a deer bladder lashed tight with pitched sinews.
The flint I carried in a pouch tied to my wrist.
I crawled with hips and belly till I came
into a place where I could squat. There I made
my first light. The water sounded fairly near
though the first spur I took was full of twists
that led me further from it. I turned back.
Now inching on a ledge with steep sloped roof,
I struck a fissure where the torrent spouted.
I whispered to the spirit, filled my lungs
and plunged.
       Swim? I doubt a salmon could
have swum it. I braced and fought for holds
in walls and ceiling to haul myself along,
still with no sign that anything but more
and wilder water lay ahead, a chance
a man must take. Half-drowned, I reached a sweep
and lay there spewing out my lungs and caught between
terror of the dark and the solid feel
of rock beneath me. I hoped the bladder
still was staunch but dared not open it until
I knew my hands were dry. When at last I twirled
the firestick and coaxed the wick to flame,
I saw the place was far too open
to waste good work on.
    I edged my way along a slit so barred
by stone icicles that I would have given up
when, almost now in reach, I saw the wall
that I have known since childhood
yet never seen before. I saw it now
even to the scratches other men,
knowing the place for what it was, had made
ages before me. Some of their animals were not

like ours—one hairy beast with two horns on his snout
was half glazed over by a layer of stone-ice.
Many of them were drawn overlapping others—
as mine would sprawl on theirs. None of them
was anything the size that I intended.

The stone was even-grained, would take flint clean,
and yet not soft enough to flake with time.
Pressing my back against the other wall
to have full arm-room, I sketched him in—
a bear as big as living. I worked fast,
paused only when the need was to renew
the wick and tallow. First I got the spine—
that line where limberness and strength
of any living beast is—cut firmly,
the head scaled in and forelegs placed
before the tallow failed.
                    Spilling down the torrent,
then guided most by slithering in my own tracks,
I found my way out—into moonlight. The sun,
it seemed, had set twice since I left.
                    Ate and slept but, lest
the bear-feel be dimmed in me, did not go in
to either of my women.
I told no one where I had been nor why.

Next day I packed another bladder, taking
a good supply of moss and tallow, honey and nuts,
and other, heavier, newly beveled flints.
As a last thought, I went to see old Kill-Bear.
"Look like?" he puffed. "A bear? Why, you've seen bears
since you were a baby." (And drawn them too,
he might have said, since I could scratch earth
with a stick.) "Come now, you've seen those I killed.
Look like? Well, they've got hair all over them.
Stub tails, big paws and heads and lots of teeth."

I left the old fool bawling after me:
"Hey, you ain't found one, have you? You're supposed
to tell me if you have. Don't you go trying
to get my job by killing it yourself!"

I found the cave was easier going this time,
but the torrent sucked and swirled up to the ceiling.
I moved half into it to test its tug.
It grabbed me, pulled me under. The bladder buoying me,
I found a shallow dome that let my nose just clear
the water. Strange, there with death so sure, I thought
not for my women nor their young but for the bear
that I would leave unfinished. Him I commended
to the spirits of the dark.
                          Slowly the water
ebbed below my chin and then my shoulders.
It rose again and then as sudden fell.
                    I was on a rock shelf.
I had slept. The bladder was still with me.
The roar was gone, the water gurgled like a brook.

The new flints bit well. To give him weight,
I undergouged the belly and hind quarters.
A natural bulge I fashioned into head.
I gave him teeth and claws. Then last of all,
he took on eyes and nostrils. When he began to breathe,
I stopped and snuffed the wick, safe in his
protection, slept.
                  Waking and making light the last time,
I scratched a spear mark on his flank as we were taught—
so shallow though that he would never feel it,
made him an offering of honey, nuts and tallow,
ate some myself. The lamp and flints I left there.

Heft, strength, the saddle and the soles,
the rambling appetite, fur, the rolling amble,

the curious, investigating "Whoof!"
the clatter of unretracting claws, the bear-play—
sliding on their rumps down clay banks into puddles,
standing erect and balancing vines across their noses—
patience to wait with poised paw
                on a rock among the rapids
to snatch the salmon as they leap,
the good
bear-smell of being bears
        are what I had tried to make the flint say
        on the cavern wall.

        Ferocity and gentleness . . .

Your bear is one great fool and so is man!
I have seen a naked child in pigtails,
squealing her delight,
chase a full-grown bear splashing across the meadow—
and a half-grown cub stand up and brave
a dozen hunters with javelins and torches.

    Bison are better eating
    and their hides tan easier
    but you can't laugh at a bison.

Beside the profound, absolute
dark of caves, our night seems noon.
Even beneath a starless sky,
the eye makes out bulk and shapes,
but in winding scapes of underground
where no sun's light has ever shone,
finger may touch the lash
of open eye unseen.

           There
in that total lack of light

is where my bear is.
No one will ever see him
but he still
is there.

High Abyss

> ". . . où flottaison blème
> Et ravie, un noyé pensif parfois descend."
> Rimbaud

File in stiffly from the wing, bow to the audience
they make believe isn't there, spread tails,
take seats, set to tuning, open scores:
    STRING QUARTET IN C♯ MINOR
        Opus 131
The lumpy, bald one with the goldfish lips
    raises his bow.

      Flotsam,
        noyé ravi,
I have been an instant-lifespan borne,
flashflooded, up into an abyss,
caught by shrill serene tumult
      into cyclone depths beyond me,
effaced by vision more intense
than I could ever know,
lulled by a wild accord of warring energies.

      Noyé pensif,
I have come back having grasped perhaps as much

as a lightning bug, clinging through a storm
to a leaf's underside,
might understand by fellow-feeling
of the lightning stroke that in a single blast
has ripped the elm trunk all its length.

Four sweating men are drawing horsehair
across squills of lamb gut and silver wire—
and give the resin credit too; it makes the squawk.

Delirious order
of the march of suns and comets.
In this expanse of tranquil ecstasy that made
"cold tears of anguish and terror
seep painfully through [Berlioz's] eyelids,"
if I say "prayer," I have blown the word
        for ever use again.
If I say "grief," what of the tremulous exultation,
the clamorous glee, triumphant resignation?

And what of the fifth movement,
the lusty, raucous dawn,
gross repetitions, pizzicati plucked on frayed nerves
redeemed only by the reveilles answering back and forth
over the waking town . . . babble of the marketplace?
                Hate its relentless jangle until
you come, to your surprise, to love it?

And the desolate resolve that breaks in close upon it?
And the headlong order of the finale?

Four by now—the quartet counts seven movements with
no pause between and tailcoats are warm—
much sweat-sodden men
are sawing resined horsehair
against strips of lambs' intestines.

       Beyond . . .
"Beyond beauty," as Wagner said
Beyond analogy   Coherence beyond coherence
Locus beyond space-time continuum
                (Paddy . . . Mim . . .)
Dawn beyond all limit of horizon.

Four men bow woodenly, file off the stage
taking their instruments, leaving the scores
on racks behind them.

Notes

Asbestos Phoenix and Maximum Security Ward included the following notes by Guthrie.

Pages 42-50, "Pattern for a Brocade Shroud," Part I: *Watteau*: The reference is to his *Embarquement pour Cythère, Jugement de Paris*, and the *fêtes galantes*. *Autumn crocus*: A stemless perennial with pale-lavender flowers. It grows wild in meadows in parts of Europe. *Norns*: In Teutonic myth, these demigoddesses, corresponding to the Parcae, weave the weirds of both men and gods. *The graces*: A game in which the players, each using two wands, toss a small hoop, often covered with velvet, back and forth. Part VII: *Tobyhanna*: An army post where National Guard artillery units mustered into federal service at the time of the American punitive expedition into Mexico were trained. *Monastir*: A city in Macedonia. In 1917 the French forces, consisting largely of colonial troops, tried to break through the Germans, Austrians, and Bulgars positioned in a semicircle of mountains above the town. *Palmes académiques*: Every few years the French government insists on awarding me this decoration, with or without rosette. I can't imagine why. *Dolmen*: These megalithic burial chambers (*circa* 2300-1000 B.C.) usually consist of a capstone supported by a number of side slabs planted vertically in the earth. They are found throughout most of France. In a cemetery at Meudon, in the suburbs of Paris, is a dolmen that was dismantled and transported from Brittany to serve as a family tomb. *Vézère*: Before cocacolonization came along, the Vézère was one of the loveliest of rivers. Of late years, many of its fine medieval bridges have been replaced by cement and iron ones.

Pages 61-62, "They Danced": *Saint Budóc*: Most of the popular Breton saints are not to be found in orthodox hagiographies. Saint Budóc immigrated from Ireland to Brittany on a floating stone. Saint Cornély, patron of horned animals, fled from Rome with his two pet oxen. When the Roman soldiers who were pursuing him cornered him against the sea near Carnac, he turned them into the great alignments of granite menhirs that still stand there. Saint Winok'h was wont to go on such homicidal drunks that he had to be kept chained up in his cell. As for Saint Melio, he was a King who was murdered by his brother in 538 A.D.; the splendid parish close of Guimiliau commemorates him. *Urchins:* The reference is mainly to sea-urchins (*oursins*) and obliquely to an elderly Mr.-Chips-like Englishman who used to startle new acquaintances by innocently confessing that the reason he chose to live in Marseilles was that he "so adored the urchins," meaning the echinoderms, locally esteemed as a delicacy, that are sold and eaten generally *sur place*, along the quai of the Vieux Port. He lived with a stocky girl named Gasparde, who looked like an unbathed bison. She chose his ties, shined his shoes and, all Anglican that he was, took him to Mass every Sunday.

Pages 85 ff., Maximum Security Ward: Maximum Security Ward is a single poem composed of a number of movements which, as often as not, are fully comprehensible only by their relation to other movements and to the poem as a whole. GLOSSARY: *Broceliande:* In this vast forest of Brittany the young Vivian laid a spell on her elderly lover Merlin that was to keep him forever captive and visible only to herself. *Viollet-le-duc* (1814-1879): Architect who restored many medieval monuments of France. One of the chimeras, often miscalled "gargoyles," with which he decorated the towers of Notre-Dame is a favorite subject of postcards of Paris. *'titer-marsher:* German hand-grenade of W.W. I, shaped like a potato-masher. *Christos, christoi:* Pronounced to rhyme respectively with "lees toss" and "lees toy." *Paul Burlin* (1886-1969): American painter living in Montparnasse during the 1920's. *Arnaut Daniel:* One of the greatest of the troubadours (circa 1190). He was greatly admired by Dante and is said to have been a favorite poet of Richard Coeur-de-Lion. *Hudimesnil:* The reference is to a mystic experience of the hero of Proust's novel. Not being able to interpret the message that this clump of trees seems to be trying to convey to him, he feels as heartbroken as if he had betrayed a dead friend or denied a god.

* * *

EDITOR'S TEXTUAL NOTES. The texts of *Graffiti* (New York: Macmillan, 1959), *Asbestos Phoenix* (New York: Funk & Wagnalls, 1968), and *Maximum Security Ward* (New York: Farrar, Straus & Giroux, 1970), have been followed with minor corrections. Mechanical errors have been corrected silently—e.g., such typographical errors as "chains" instead of "chairs" in "Variations on a Threne for Tristan Tzara," fifth line from the end, page 75, or various problems of indentation in *Maximum Security Ward*. The "corrections" in the following notes are of Guthrie's obviously unintentional misspellings. In this regard, it should perhaps be pointed out that on page 119 "calvary" instead of "cavalry" is correct, as is "Perishing" instead of "Pershing."

Graffiti:

Page 7, "Dead, How to Become It": "steles" changed to "slabs" (part 2, 1. 13), based on Guthrie's change in his copy of *Graffiti; page 8*: "Terruel" corrected to "Teruel" (part 4, 1. 7). *Page 16*, "Postlude: For Goya": The text follows the version in *Asbestos Phoenix*. The most substantive change involves the last sentence, which in *Graffiti* reads "We have won if we can believe / that this is not an end."

Asbestos Phoenix:

Page 52, "Unveiling a Statue to a One-Time Poet": "slante" corrected to "slainte" (1. 3).

Maximum Security Ward:

Pages 87-96: Four poems in *Maximum Security Ward* appear also in *Asbestos Phoenix*, in a different order and with slightly different texts. They are "Red-headed Interne [sic] Taking Notes," "Via Crucis," "Elegy for Mélusine from the Intensive Care Ward," and "Scene: A Bedside in the Witches' Kitchen." *Page 95*, "sphygnomanometer" corrected to "sphygmomanometer" (1. 15). *Page 117*,

"The Prayers": German quotation corrected from "Im Aufang" to "Im Anfang." *Page 142,* "The Surf": the Spanish "Finisterre" changed to the French "Finistère" (1. 6), based on a correction in Guthrie's hand on the galleys of the 1970 volume. *Page 180,* "People Walking": "Terruel" corrected to "Teruel" (third stanza, 1. 10). *Page 183,* "Amó" corrected to "Amò." *Page 186,* " 'And the Evening and the Morning' ": "had" corrected to "has" in the opening line of the stage directions. These are somewhat confusing, since it is only in the next poem, "Judgment Day," that the "Voices" speak. Guthrie reversed the position of the two poems—as they appeared in a 1966-67 typewritten draft of *Maximum Security Ward*—without, apparently, adapting the stage directions.

*   *   *

List of full pages on which the last line concludes a stanza (final stanzas excepted): 12, 14, 16, 26, 40, 46, 52, 55, 64, 75, 87, 88, 99, 101, 109, 112, 121, 132, 135, 138, 151, 157, 158, 166, 167, 172, 178, 181, 188, 189, 190, 197.

A Tentative*
Ramon Guthrie Chronology

1896-1916

14 January 1896, Raymon Hollister Guthrie is born in New York City (he claimed his birth certificate said 13 January but his mother said 14 January) to Harry and Ella May Guthrie (née Hollister). Supposedly named after a singer, Raymon Moore, he later discards both the "y" and his middle name. He has an older sister, Eleanor, probably born in 1889. In 1898 or so Harry decamps with another woman and vanishes from sight. (Guthrie said his father eventually remarried and that he saw him only once again, in 1905, for a few minutes. He believed his father died in 1910 in an unsuccessful attempt to prevent another's suicide by gas.)

Years of grinding poverty follow. Mrs. Guthrie moves to Hartford and supports her children with difficulty, running a boarding house, working as a dressmaker, Christian Science practitioner, and manicurist, etc. Due to her poor health the children probably spend a brief period in an orphanage when Guthrie is about five (despite his mother's Connecticut relatives). After completing grammar school, Guthrie is unable, for financial reasons, to accept a scholarship to the Hartford Art School. He works at odd jobs and in the Underwood typewriter factory and flunks out of night school. From 1912 to 1915, however, he manages to attend the Northfield Mount Hermon School (in Massachusetts) for part of each year. Several of his poems appear in *The Hermonite*. (See "The Archangel Michael" for Mount Hermon's evangelical flavor.)

In 1915 Mrs. Guthrie has her first stroke and moves in with a sister near New Haven. Guthrie goes to work for the Winchester Repeating Arms factory in New Haven, at this time busy filling war orders. He works on the night shift straightening draw punches.

*Much of this biographical information comes from the poet himself, whose memory delighted his friends with its creativity and genius for self-revision.

After another stroke early in 1916 his mother commits suicide in the charity ward of the New Haven Hospital. (See "Fiercer Than Evening Wolves" for details of this early period.)

1916-22

War and coming of age in France. Guthrie decides not to return to Mount Hermon in the fall and instead enlists in the 10th Connecticut Field Artillery. (Eleanor, whom Guthrie remembered as given to temper tantrums, has married. She and her brother are essentially estranged from 1916 on. Guthrie said she later married Lt. Col. Charles Wallington Furlong and was a friend of Mary Baker Eddy.) In December, however, he sails for France as a volunteer with the American Field Service and is an ambulance driver with the Eighth Army on the Western Front for several months and then with the Armée de l'Orient in the Balkans.

Returning to France, Guthrie joins the U.S. Army's Aviation Section Signal Corps and trains as an observer. (He said he was afraid the war would be over before he could complete training as a pilot.) He walks away from a spectacular plane crash, which results in bouts of amnesia (see " 'Visse, Scrisse, Amò' ") and various nervous disorders, among them acusis—intolerance of loud noise—and acute attacks of anxiety and panic. (The crash is severe enough to entitle him to a disability pension.) He is assigned to the Eleventh Bombing Squadron and participates in a disastrous raid over La Chaussée in which an incompetent major sends the planes aloft with machine guns out of order and without a fighter escort. Guthrie and his pilot, the only survivors, are forced to watch the other planes shot down (see "Death with Pants On"). Fortunately, their machine gun is working, and Guthrie shoots down two enemy fighters and survives to become a successful formation leader and to shoot down two more. He is awarded two citations, one of them the Silver Star. While serving in the army he discovers Paris and his future wife, Marguerite Maurey from Nancy. At the end of the war he takes a course in French civilization at the Sorbonne, but in the summer of 1919 he is shipped back to the States.

After several hospitalizations (see his novel *Parachute*, based on a hospital for convalescent airmen in Cooperstown) and a few months' work as an insurance investigator, he returns to France. His poems appear in Norman Fitts's little magazine *S4N* (which Fitts had founded along with Guthrie, Stephen Vincent Benét, Roger Sessions, Thornton Wilder, and others), and in *Paris Review: The Illustrated American Magazine in France.* He studies political science at Toulouse under a disability pension, earning two special degrees for foreigners, the *license* and *doctorat en droit*, in 1921 and 1922; but he continues his literary studies and poetry, including translations from the Provençal.

1922-29

The flourishing of a poet-novelist-translator. On 8 April 1922 Guthrie marries Marguerite in Toulouse. They move to Paris, and during 1922-23 he works on a semi-autobiographical novel, "Philip" (unpublished except for one chapter, "Marchand d'habits," in the January-February 1923 issue of *S4N*). He writes poetry, follows courses at the Sorbonne in Old French and Provençal, is rumored to have become one of Otto Rank's patients, and participates in the literary and artistic life centered in Montparnasse. (See "Ezra Pound in Paris and Elsewhere," "Montparnasse," and "For Approximately the Same Reason.")

The Guthries return to the United States in 1923, also the year of his first collection of poems, *Trobar Clus* (the first book put out by the S4N Society). Malcolm Cowley introduces Guthrie to the avant-garde literary scene in New York, but Guthrie's search for a job takes him to the University of Arizona, where he teaches French language and literature courses from 1924 to 1926. (See "The Clown: Hurrah for the Petrified Forest" and "There Are Those.")

In 1926 the Guthries return to France and the eminently congenial expatriate milieu—partly at the instigation of Sinclair Lewis, whose collaboration with and dependence on Guthrie absorb much of the poet's time and energy over the next decades. Besides *Trobar Clus* (1923), Guthrie publishes his novel *Marcabrun* (1926); another collection of poems (*A World Too Old*, 1927); a translation of Bernard Faÿ's *The Revolutionary Spirit in France and America* (1927); a second novel (*Parachute*, 1928); and the risqué narrative poem *The Legend of Ermengarde* (1929). That year the Guthries return to the United States, probably for economic reasons.

1930-63

The Dartmouth years and relative poetic silence. From 1930 to 1963, except for a stint in the O.S.S. during World War Two in France and Algiers as liaison with the French Resistance (for which he is also cited)—see "Fragment of a Travelogue" and "For Approximately the Same Reason"—Guthrie teaches full time at Dartmouth College (Hanover, New Hampshire), specializing in Proust. He makes his home across the border in Norwich, Vermont, and returns to France as frequently as possible during vacations and sabbaticals, often to paint rather than write. (He once figured that he had lived 16 years in France.) He is made an *Officier d'Académie* in 1949 and an *Officier dans l'ordre des Palmes académiques* in 1963 (see "Pattern for a Brocade Shroud").

His scholarly enterprises include occasional articles, among them discussions of his close relationship with Lewis; a number of reviews—especially for the *New York Herald Tribune Book Review*; the preparation of two anthologies (with George E. Diller): *French Literature and Thought Since the Revolution* (1942) and *Prose and Poetry of Modern France* (1964); and two 1947 translations: *The Republic of Silence*, compiled by A. J. Liebling, and *The Other Kingdom*, by David Rousset.

Guthrie, however, does not abandon poetry entirely during this period. In 1933 The Arts Press (Hanover) brings out his *Scherzo from a Poem To Be Entitled The Proud City*; in 1938 he writes his long, anti-Fascist, unpublished poem "Instead of Abel"; he participates in the Thursday evening meetings of poets living in the area (among them Richard Eberhart, Bink Noll, Thomas and Vera Vance, and Alexander Laing and—especially—his wife Dilys); and he puts together the manuscript of *Graffiti* (1959) for M. L. Rosenthal, then poetry advisor at Macmillan, who has also published some of his poems in *The Nation*. As his retirement from full-time teaching approaches (1963—although he teaches through the fall semester of 1965), his poetic output increases markedly.

1964-73

Guthrie's last years and his final poetic flourishing, which takes place against the backdrop of his escalating medical problems and the Vietnam War. (He vehemently opposes the war—see "Some of Us Must Remember" and "Scherzo for a Dirge"—and in 1965 returns his World War One Silver Star to President Johnson in protest.)

His first operation for cancer of the bladder takes place in the summer of 1966, and he starts on *Maximum Security Ward*. He is well enough in 1967 to give some readings in France and to spend time at Yaddo, but is very ill at the beginning of 1968 and starts a course of cobalt therapy. Emile Capouya accepts *Asbestos Phoenix* for Funk & Wagnalls in January. Despite his physical condition, Guthrie spends late spring and summer in Paris. (See "Boul' Miche, May 1968.") Back home he races to correct the galleys of *Asbestos Phoenix* before undergoing surgery to remove his colon, which has been severely damaged by the cobalt treatment. Despite the dangerous operation and massive transfusions, he recovers enough to see *Asbestos Phoenix* in print and to return to Paris in the summer of 1969, but there he hemorrhages badly and ends up in the American Hospital. (See "The Dutch Head Nurse.")

He is shipped home in such poor condition that he is not expected to recover, but with *Maximum Security Ward* not quite finished he insists on being taken off pain-killers so that he can complete it. By October it is at the typist's, and Robert Giroux accepts it in the spring of 1970 for Farrar, Straus & Giroux. From now until his death Guthrie is essentially house– and hospital–bound. More operations follow, and he is too sick in May of 1970 (he is in fact unconscious for most of six weeks) to accept the Marjorie Peabody Waite Award of the National Institute of Arts and Letters in person, and Cowley accepts for him. But by June 1971 he is well enough to attend the Dartmouth commencement ceremonies, during which he is elected an honorary member of Phi Beta Kappa and receives the Litt. D. Compounding his surgical problems, however, are Parkinson's Disease, asthma, double vision, and eventually hallucinations. He is hospitalized for much of 1972 and 1973.

22 November 1973, Thanksgiving Day, having finally suc-

ceeded in getting himself released from the hospital but not from his unrelenting physical and mental torment, Guthrie very probably takes an overdose of a prescription drug. He dies at Mary Hitchcock Memorial Hospital in Hanover in the afternoon. His grave, marked by a miniature dolmen, overlooks Norwich. Marguerite dies three years later.

Index of Titles and Opening Words